EXPLORING

German

THIRD EDITION

Joan G. Sheeran

Consultant
Wolfgang S. Kraft

EMC
Publishing

ST. PAUL • LOS ANGELES

Illustrations
Lachina Publishing
Rolin Graphics

Design & Composition
Lisa Beller

Cover Design
Leslie Anderson

Production Editor
Amy McGuire

Care has been taken to verify the accuracy of information presented in this book. However, the authors, editors, and publisher cannot accept responsibility for Web, e-mail, newsgroup, or chat room subject matter content, or for consequences from application of the information in this book, and make no warranty, expressed or implied, with respect to its content.

Photo Credits

Archivo Iconografico, S.A./Corbis: 126 (top left)
Arnold, Bernd: 85 (top left)
Art Archive/Corbis: 184 (bottom), 185
Associated Press/Axel Seidermann: 226 (top)
Associated Press/Fritz Reiss: 225 (bottom)
Austrian National Tourist Office: 45 (bottom), 48 (top), 79 (left), 183 (top left)
Bettmann/Corbis: 224 (bottom)
Brücke Museum, Berlin, Germany/The Bridgeman Art Library: 127 (bottom)
Bundesbildstelle Berlin: 226 (bottom)
Corbis Royalty-Free: 13 (center), 71 (bottom right), 97 (top left), 139 (top), 195 (left & top right), 223 (bottom right), 225 (top), 235 (top left), 249 (top left), 261 (bottom left)
da Veiga, Hannah: 79 (right)
Dietz, Madeleine/Courtesy of the artist: 129 (bottom)
Digital Stock: 71 (top right), 97 (top right), 223 (top left)
Digital Vision: 97 (bottom left)
Directmedia: 126 (bottom), 127 (top)
Fassbender, Ins/Reuters/Corbis: 186 (right)
Frankfurt Tourist & Congress Board: 41 (top right), 43, 111 (center right), 223 (top right), 261 (top left), 266 (bottom left)
Fremdenverkehrsamt Saarfelden: 235 (top right)
Gästeinformation-Schliersee: viii (bottom right)
German National Tourist Office: viii (top left)
Getty Images: 71 (top left)
Hamburg Tourismus GmbH: 125, 167 (top left)
Harzer Verkehrsverband e.V.: 195 (top center)
Heyder, Felix/dpa/Corbis: 186 (left)
Historical Picture Archive/Corbis: 126 (top right)
Inter Nationes: 261 (bottom right)
Klein, Dieter: 139 (bottom left & right)
Kraft, Wolfgang: iii (bottom left & right), iv (left), ix (all), x (bottom left & right), xi (top left & center right), 1 (top left & bottom right), 13 (top right, bottom left & right), 29 (all), 97 (bottom right), 103 (bottom left & right), 111 (bottom left & right, top right), 153 (all), 158, 160 (all), 167 (top & bottom right), 174, 183 (bottom & top right), 195 (bottom center), 209 (all), 235 (center), 243 (all), 249 (bottom left & right), 253 (all), 261 (top right), 266 (top & bottom right)
Krause, Johansen/Archivo Iconografico, SA/Corbis: 224 (top)
Lasker-Schüler-Gesellschaft, Else: 225 (center)
Leipzig Tourist Service e.V.: 41 (bottom left), 44 (top), 223 (bottom left)
Nordrhein-Westfalen Tourismus e.V.: 41 (bottom right)
PhotoPaq: 85 (bottom left)
Plefmann, Gregor: 235 (bottom left)
Simson, David: iii (top right), x (top left & right), xi (bottom left), 1 (top right), 115 (bottom), 167 (bottom left), 267 (all)
Spichtinger, Herbert /zefa/Corbis: 114 (bottom)
Sturmhoefel, Horst: 67 (right), 71 (bottom left), 85 (bottom right), 111 (top left)
Swiss-Image GmbH: 48 (bottom)
Switzerland Tourism: 103 (top right), 235 (bottom right)
TH-Foto/zefa/Corbis: 115 (top)
Tourism-Marketing GmbH Baden-Württemberg: 167 (bottom center)
Tourismus Marketing Gesellschaft Sachsen mbH: iv (right), 44 (bottom), 46, 59, 183 (bottom left), 184 (top), 249 (top right)
Tourismusverband Lieser-Maltatal: xi (top right)
Tourismusverband Mecklenburg-Vorpommern: 195 (bottom right)
Tourismusverband Romantisches Franken: v (all)
Touristikverband Schleswig-Holstein e.V.: 85 (top right)
Verkehrsamt Lichtenfels: 103 (top left)
Verkehrsamt Murnau: 41 (top left)
Verlag Papeterie GmbH: viii (top right)
Votteler, Jutta/Courtesy of German Art Company: 129 (top)
Walker Art Center: 128
Zürich Tourism: viii (bottom left), 45 (top)

We have made every effort to trace the ownership of all copyrighted material and to secure permission from copyright holders. In the event of any question arising as to the use of any material, we will be pleased to make the necessary corrections in future printings. Thanks are due to the aforementioned authors, publishers and agents for permission to use the materials indicated. The publisher would like to thank the various tourist offices that gave permission to use realia in this book.

Softcover Edition: ISBN 978-0-82193-484-5

Hardcover Edition: ISBN 978-0-82194-041-9

© 2008 by EMC Publishing, LLC
875 Montreal Way
St. Paul, MN 55102
E-mail: educate@emcp.com
Web site: www.emcp.com

17 16 15 14 13 12 11 10 09 08 XXX   2 3 4 5 6 7 8 9 10

Introduction

Congratulations on starting your exploration of German! As you begin your study, you are joining thousands of other young people who, like you, are curious about other cultures and are fascinated by the idea of speaking a different language. German is the perfect choice for you! Since the German language is distantly related to English, you will see many familiar words. Also, since the Germanic traditions of German-speaking settlers have helped shape American culture, you will realize how very similar our respective cultures are. As you begin this exciting new experience, think about connecting with young people all around the world who use German as a common language!

Did you know that. . .?

- more than one fourth of the population in the United States claims German ancestry?

- German is the world's largest exporter and a major trading partner of the United States?

- over 200 million Europeans speak German as their first language?

- German is an international language in the fields of technology, chemistry, medicine, music, philosophy, and art?

- more Germans travel per capita than any other national group in the world? You're likely to meet them everywhere!

- one out of every ten books published in the world is written in German?

- a knowledge of German improves your understanding of English? German language students are likely to score higher on college entrance exams than other students!

The German language of today is actually a living descendent of an original language family called Indo-European. German is a distant linguistic cousin of many other European languages today such as Polish, Welsh, English, Norwegian, French, Spanish, and Greek. German contains similarities to French, and it has many words derived from Latin. Your own language, English, originated from German. For all these reasons German is truly an international language!

Have you ever heard of the word *cognate*? This is a word from another language that may *look* and *sound* similar to an English word. Can you figure out what these German words are? Take a good look and guess!

Glas   Maschine   Haus   Finger   Rose   blau   braun   grün

Now try these sentences:

1. Die Musik ist laut.
2. Der Schuh ist braun.
3. Das Haus ist weiß.
4. Das Gras ist grün.
5. Das Glas ist kaputt.

Your teacher can tell you whether you guessed correctly or not. Chances are, you did VERY WELL!

There is a section toward the end of each unit with symbols. Each symbol represents a word or expression in German. This learning method is called "Symtalk" (symbols + talking). You will be asked to "read" the sentences and then to engage in a directed dialogue with a partner or describe a scene. When you write sentences in this section, you will be talking about the characters shown below. You can refer back to this page as often as you like until you learn the names of all the characters.

You are now ready to get on the bandwagon and join the millions of other speakers of German. As your friends in Mexico, Bolivia, Canada, Japan, Italy, Hungary, Russia, Poland, and France would agree, learning the German language is cool, easy, and also very important in the business world today. Have fun with German! *Viel Spaß!*

Symtalk Characters

Daniel	**Silvia**	**Hiko**
Anton	**Brigitte**	**Thomas**

Table of Contents

Exploring

... countries and cities

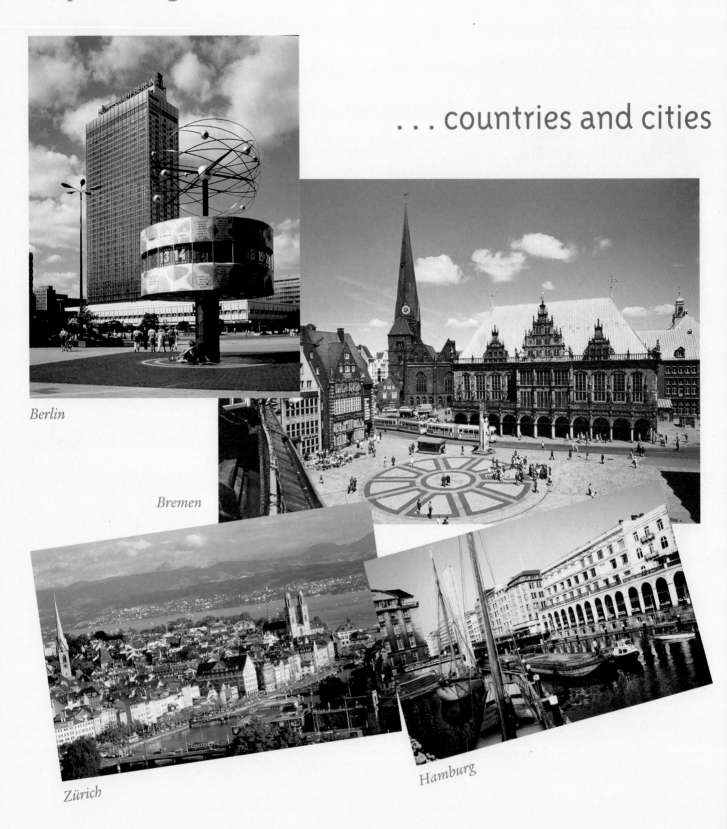

Berlin

Bremen

Zürich

Hamburg

. . . language

. . . and culture.

DEUTSCHLAND

DÄNEMARK

OSTSEE

Sylt

Nordfriesische Inseln

Flensburg

NORDSEE

Fehmarn

Rügen

Usedom

Kiel

Schleswig-Holstein

Rostock

Mecklenburg-

Lübeck

Schwerin

Neubrandenburg

Ostfriesische Inseln

Cuxhaven

Hamburg

Hamburg

Vorpommern

Wilhelmshaven

Bremerhaven

Elbe

Bremen

Bremen

Oldenburg

NIEDERLANDE

Niedersachsen

POLEN

Oder

Weser

Osnabrück

Hannover

Wolfsburg

Brandenburg

Berlin

Berlin

Münster

Braunschweig

Magdeburg

Potsdam

Spree

Frankfurt

Bielefeld

Hildesheim

Salzgitter

Sachsen-

Brandenburg

Recklinghausen

Weser

Göttingen

Anhalt

Dessau

Elbe

Cottbus

Neiße

Duisburg

Nordrhein-

Westfalen

Dortmund

Halle

Leipzig

Görlitz

Essen

Mönchen-

Düsseldorf

Kassel

Weimar

Jena

Sachsen

gladbach

Leverkusen

Eisenach

Erfurt

Gera

Dresden

Chemnitz

Aachen

Köln

Siegen

Hessen

Thüringen

Zwickau

Bonn

Rhein

BEL-

GIEN

Koblenz

TSCHECHISCHE

LUXEM-

Wiesbaden

Frankfurt

Main

Main

Bamberg

REPUBLIK

BURG

Rheinland-

Pfalz

Mainz

Offenbach

Darmstadt

Würzburg

Bayreuth

Mosel

Erlangen

Saarland

Ludwigshafen

Mannheim

Fürth

Nürnberg

Saarbrücken

Kaiserslautern

Heidelberg

Heilbronn

Rothenburg

ob der Tauber

Regensburg

Karlsruhe

Bayern

Pforzheim

Stuttgart

Donau

Ingolstadt

Donau

Passau

Rhein

Tübingen

Augsburg

FRANKREICH

Baden-

Württemberg

Ulm

München

ÖSTERREICH

Freiburg

Bodensee

Garmisch-

Partenkirchen

Berchtesgaden

Watzmann

2713

Rhein

▲ 2963

Zugspitze

SCHWEIZ

LIECHTENSTEIN

© edigol

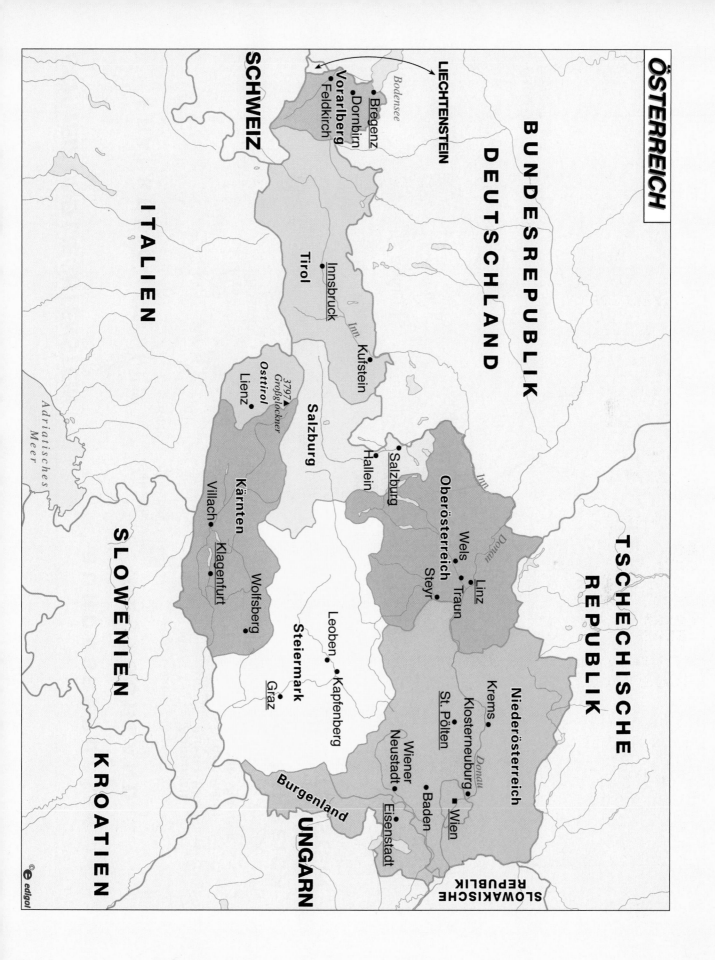

ÖSTERREICH

SCHWEIZ

BUNDESREPUBLIK
DEUTSCHLAND

LIECHTENSTEIN

Bodensee

● Bregenz
Vorarlberg
● Dornbirn
● Feldkirch

ITALIEN

Tirol
● Innsbruck

Inn

● Kufstein

3797 ▲
Großglockner

Osttirol
● Lienz

Salzburg

Hallein ●
● Salzburg

Inn

Oberösterreich
Wels ●
● Linz
● Traun
● Steyr

Donau

TSCHECHISCHE
REPUBLIK

Adriatisches
Meer

Kärnten
● Villach

● Klagenfurt

● Wolfsberg

Steiermark

Leoben ●
● Kapfenberg

● Graz

Krems ●
Niederösterreich
Klosterneuburg ●
St. Pölten ●

Donau

Wiener
Neustadt ●
● Baden
■ Wien

Eisenstadt ●

Burgenland

SLOWAKISCHE REPUBLIK

SLOWENIEN

KROATIEN

UNGARN

© edigol

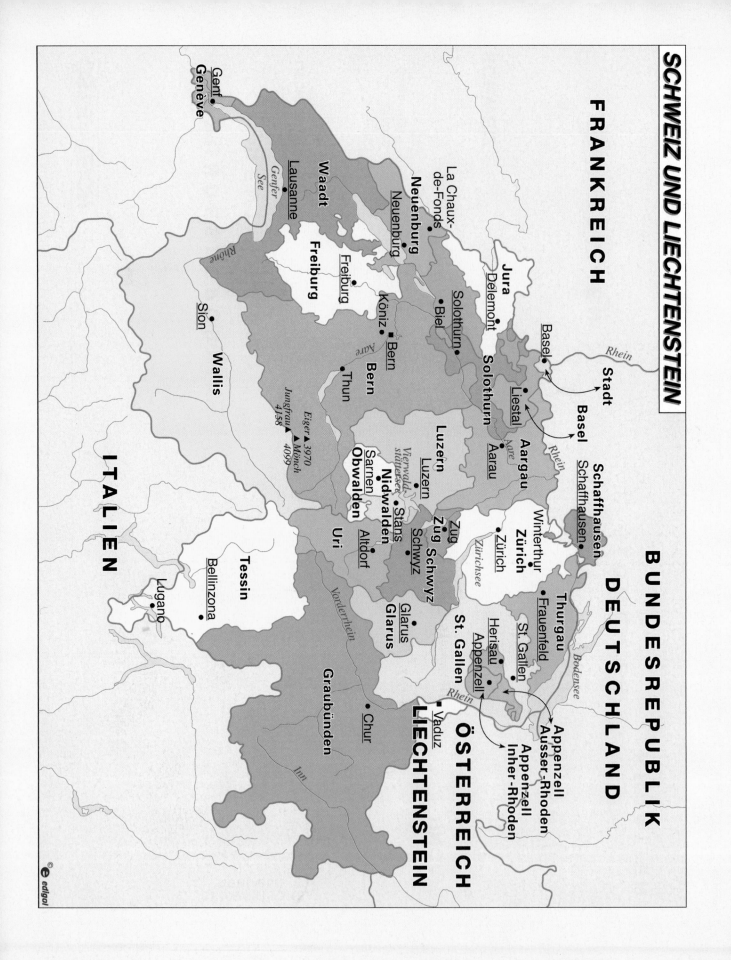

SCHWEIZ UND LIECHTENSTEIN

Unit 1

Begrüßungen und Höflichkeit
Greetings and Expressions of Courtesy

Vokabeln

Höflichkeit

Bitte.	Please.
Danke.	Thank you.
Bitte schön.	You're welcome.
Entschuldigung!	Excuse me.
Es tut mir leid.	I'm sorry.

Viel Glück!

Good luck.

Guten Morgen!	**Guten Tag!**	**Guten Abend!**	**Gute Nacht!**
Good morning.	Hello.	Good evening.	Good night.

Ja.
Yes.

Nein.
No.

Wie heißt du?
What's your name?

Ich heiße Alex.
My name is Alex.

Angenehm./Es freut mich.
I'm pleased to meet you.

Du sprichst deutsch, nicht wahr?
You speak German, don't you?

Ja. Ich spreche deutsch.
Yes. I speak German.

Wie geht's?
How are you?

Gut, danke. Und dir?
Fine, thanks. And (how are) you?

Nicht schlecht.
Not bad. All right.

Customs and Courtesy

Handshaking is not restricted to an introduction, that is, when people meet each other for the first time. Friends shake hands as a sign that they are pleased to see each other again.

When you say hello to an adult such as a teacher or a sales clerk, use the formal greeting: *Guten Tag,* Add the person's last name if you know it: *Guten Tag, Herr Schmidt! Guten Tag, Frau Meier.* Be sure to offer a handshake as a gesture of courtesy.

Tag, an informal and casual greeting, is usually said to a friend: *Tag, Andreas!*

Die Sprachen	Languages
Deutsch	German
Arabisch	Arabic
Chinesisch	Chinese
Französisch	French
Englisch	English
Italienisch	Italian
Japanisch	Japanese
Portugiesisch	Portuguese
Russisch	Russian
Spanisch	Spanish

Extra Vokabeln

Mädchennamen
Girls' names

Ich heiße. . .

Antje	Leonie
Beate	Marie
Bettina	Nele
Claudia	Petra
Diana	Ruth
Elisabeth	Sabine
Gabriele	Susanne
Heike	Vanessa
Johanna	
Julia	**Das Mädchen**
Katharina	**heißt Katharina.**
Laura	*The girl's name is Katharina.*

Jungennamen
Boys' names

Ich heiße. . .

Alexander	Lukas
Andreas	Maximilian
Benjamin	Niklas
Daniel	Paul
Dieter	Rainer
Eberhard	Stefan
Florian	Simon
Günther	Tim
Heiko	
Jochen	**Der Junge heißt**
Karsten	**Paul.**
Leon	*The boy's name is Paul.*

Übungen

A **Wähle das nicht Zutreffende!** *(Choose the word or expression that is different from all the rest.)*

1. Ja.	Angenehm.	Es freut mich.	Guten Tag!
2. Bis morgen!	Auf Wiedersehen!	Entschuldigung!	Bis später!
3. Gute Nacht!	Viel Glück!	Guten Tag!	Guten Abend!
4. Bitte.	Danke.	Tag!	Bitte schön.
5. Deutsch	Englisch	Japanisch	Nein

B **Wähle nur Mädchennamen!** *(Choose only girls' names.)*

1. Claudia
2. Heiko
3. Karsten
4. Bettina
5. Ruth
6. Heike
7. Simon
8. Niklas
9. Sabine
10. Florian

C **Beantworte die Fragen auf Deutsch! Schreib deine Antworten!** *(Answer the questions in German. Write your answers.)*

1. Sprichst du deutsch?

   _____

2. Wie heißt du?

   _____

3. Wie geht's?

   _____

D **Schreib zu jeder Abbildung einen Ausdruck auf Deutsch!** *(Write in German an expression that corresponds to each illustration.)*

1. _____

2.  _____

3.  _____

4.  _____

5.  _____

6. _____

7. _____

E **Kurze Antworten auf Deutsch, bitte.** *(Short answers in German, please.)*

1. How do you greet someone in the morning?

    _____

2. How do you greet someone in the evening?

    _____

3. What do you say after meeting someone?

    _____

4. How do you wish someone luck?

    _____

5. How would you finish the following sentence?

    Ich spreche _____.

6. Would *Tag*, an informal greeting, generally be used to greet Robert, a friend, or Herr Weber, a gentleman?

    _____

7. Is Beate a name for *ein Junge*?

    _____

8. Answer this question: *Wie heißt du?*

_____

9. What is one expression to say good-bye? _____.

10. *Ja* is the opposite of what word? _____.

F   **Ergänze den Dialog auf Deutsch! Schreib deine Antworten!** *(Complete the dialogues in German. Write your answers.)*

1. TANJA: Tag! Ich heiße Tanja. Und du? *(And you?)*

    LUKAS: _____

2. GÜNTHER: Wie geht's, Leonie?

    LEONIE: _____

3. NIKLAS: Sprichst du deutsch, Bernd?

    BERND: Ja, _____

G   **Zum Sprechen. Talk with a classmate but pretend to meet for the first time. Act out a simple introduction.**

H   **Du bist dran!** *(It's your turn.)* **Was weißt du auf Deutsch?** *(What do you know in German?)*

1. Shake hands as you say hello to a friend.
2. Wave and say good-bye to a friend.
3. Name at least five boys' names and five girls' names.
4. Say that you speak English.

Sprichwort

Höflichkeit ist Trumpf.
Courtesy is power.

Lebendige Sprache

1

2

3

Grüße aus **Wertheim**
an Main und Tauber

5

Auf Wiedersehen in
NEUSTADT
in Holstein

4

GRÜSS GOTT
im barocken
St. Johann in Tirol

6

Grüße zum Muttertag

Herzlich ... fröhlich ... liebenswert.
Einfach schön.

Sächsische Zeitung
Was uns verbindet.

I **Match each sign or photo with the most appropriate description. In this picture. . .**

1. _____
2. _____
3. _____
4. _____
5. _____
6. _____
7. _____
8. _____
9. _____

A. visitors are welcomed to this city which has many Baroque buildings.

B. friends or relatives have arrived for a stay at the hosts' house.

C. travelers driving through the city are bid farewell.

D. the person might say, "*Ich heiße Andreas.*"

E. visitors are welcome to this town.

F. greetings are sent from a town located on two rivers.

G. a person entering the room might say, "*Guten Tag!*"

H. a mother receives birthday wishes from her two children.

I. greetings are expressed for Mother's Day.

J **Look at Photo #9 and write three sentences. Imagine what each person in this photo could be saying.**

_____

_____

_____

Symtalk

K **Ergänze die richtigen Wörter auf Deutsch!** *(In the space, write the correct word in German.)*

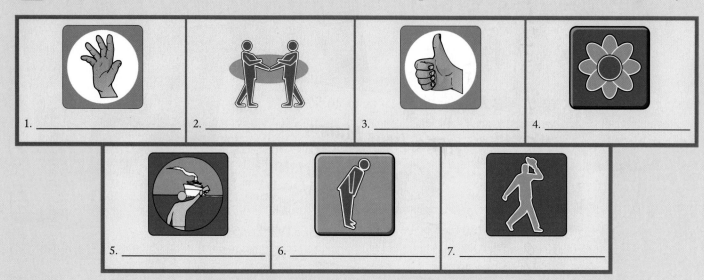

1. _____

2. _____

3. _____

4. _____

5. _____

6. _____

7. _____

L **Sag die Sätze! Dann schreib sie auf Deutsch!** *(Say the sentences, then write them in German.)*

1. _____

3. _____

2. _____

4. _____

Sieh dir die Symbole an and schreib dann die Dialoge! *(Look at the symbols, then write the dialogues.)*

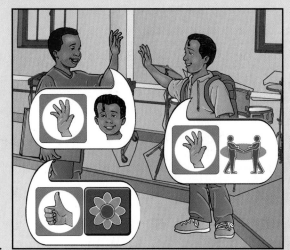

1.

2.

3.

Kreuzworträtsel

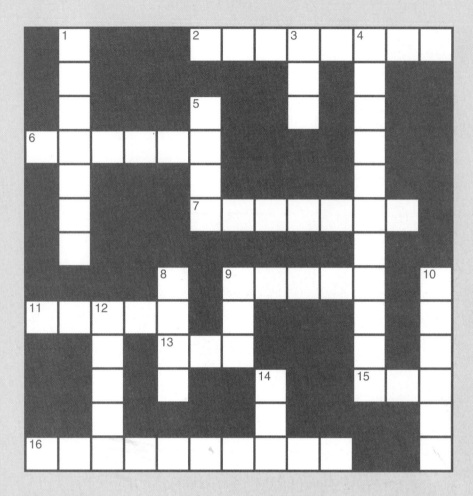

Note: ß = SS

Waagerecht

2. _____ *du deutsch?*
6. *Ich _____ Rainer.*
7. German
9. luck
11. Thank you.
13. *Höflichkeit _____ Trumpf.*
15. Hi!
16. said in the evening

Senkrecht

1. *Ich _____ englisch.*
3. _____ *heiße Melanie.*
4. courtesy
5. *Das tut mir _____.*
8. opposite of *ja*
9. opposite of *schlecht*
10. *Guten _____,* said in the morning
12. night
14. _____ *geht's?*

UNIT 2

Die Klasse und Imperative
Classroom Objects and Commands

Vokabeln

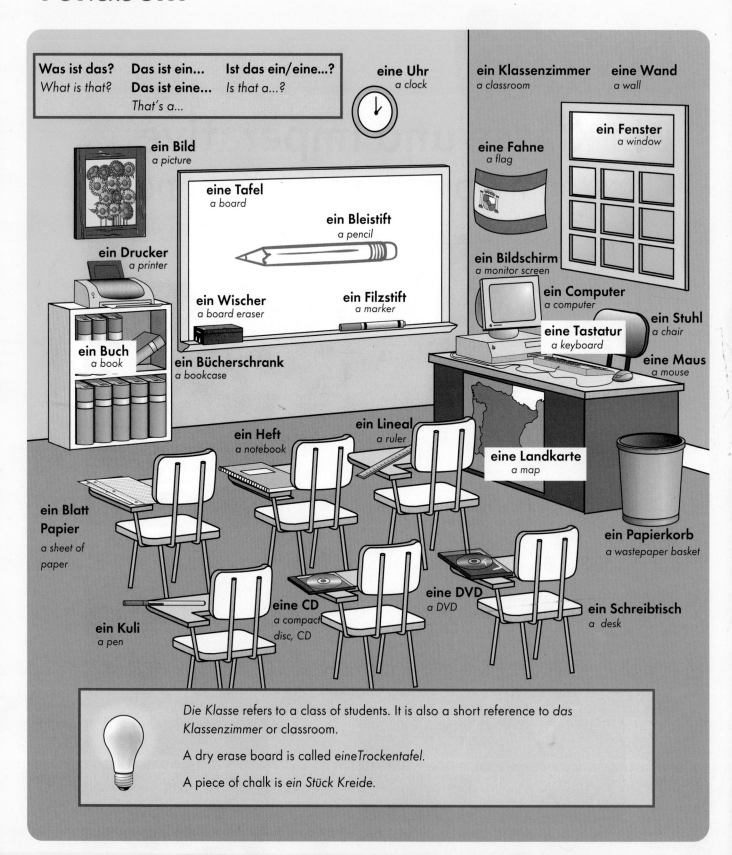

Was ist das?	Das ist ein...	Ist das ein/eine...?
What is that?	Das ist eine...	*Is that a...?*
	That's a...	

eine Uhr
a clock

ein Klassenzimmer
a classroom

eine Wand
a wall

ein Bild
a picture

eine Fahne
a flag

ein Fenster
a window

eine Tafel
a board

ein Bleistift
a pencil

ein Drucker
a printer

ein Bildschirm
a monitor screen

ein Computer
a computer

ein Wischer
a board eraser

ein Filzstift
a marker

eine Tastatur
a keyboard

ein Stuhl
a chair

ein Buch
a book

eine Maus
a mouse

ein Bücherschrank
a bookcase

ein Lineal
a ruler

ein Heft
a notebook

eine Landkarte
a map

ein Blatt Papier
a sheet of paper

ein Papierkorb
a wastepaper basket

eine CD
a compact disc, CD

eine DVD
a DVD

ein Schreibtisch
a desk

ein Kuli
a pen

Die Klasse refers to a class of students. It is also a short reference to *das Klassenzimmer* or classroom.

A dry erase board is called *eineTrockentafel*.

A piece of chalk is *ein Stück Kreide*.

Imperative in der Klasse
Classroom commands

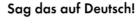

Sag das auf Deutsch!
Say it in German.

Sprich!
Speak.

Wiederhole!
Repeat.

Schreib!
Write.

Beantworte die Frage!
Answer the question.

Geh an die Tafel!
Go to the board.

Heb die Hand!
Raise your hand.

Nimm Papier heraus!
Take out paper.

Mach das Buch auf!
Open the book.

Mach das Buch zu!
Close the book.

Lies!
Read.

Hör zu!
Listen.

Zeichne ein Bild!
Draw a picture.

Ergänze die Sätze!
Complete the sentences.

Schalte den Computer an!
Turn the computer on.

Schalte den Computer aus!
Turn the computer off.

Extra Vokabeln

faxen *to send a fax*	**surfen** *to surf*	**kopieren** *to copy*
eine E-Mail senden *to send an e-mail*	**drucken** *to print*	**ein Videospiel spielen** *to play a video game*

Übungen

A Your teacher will say at random the words for 25 classroom objects. After you hear the first word, find it in the list below and write "1" in the space provided. The second word you hear will be marked "2," etc.

_____ eine Tafel

_____ ein Lineal

_____ eine CD

_____ ein Kuli

_____ ein Buch

_____ eine Landkarte

_____ ein Papierkorb

_____ ein Drucker

_____ eine Fahne

_____ eine Tastatur

_____ ein Bild

_____ ein Stuhl

_____ ein Computer

_____ ein Blatt Papier

_____ ein Filzstift

_____ ein Bleistift

_____ ein Heft

_____ eine Maus

_____ eine Uhr

_____ ein Bücherschrank

_____ ein Wischer

_____ ein Fenster

_____ ein Bildschirm

_____ ein Schreibtisch

_____ eine DVD

B Look around your own classroom as you answer these questions.

1. Do you have *ein Blatt Papier* on your desk?

_____

2. Where is your *Fahne*?

_____

3. How many *Fenster* does your room have?

_____

4. Is the *Drucker* near the computer?

_____

5. Are there many *Bücher* in the *Bücherschrank?*

_____

 Schreib den deutschen Namen von jedem Objekt! *(Write the German name for each object. Don't forget to write the indefinite article—ein or eine—before the noun.)*

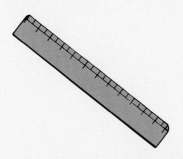

1. _____

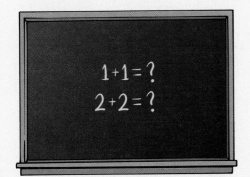

2. _____

3. _____

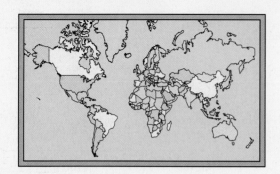

4. _____

5. _____

6. _____

7. _____

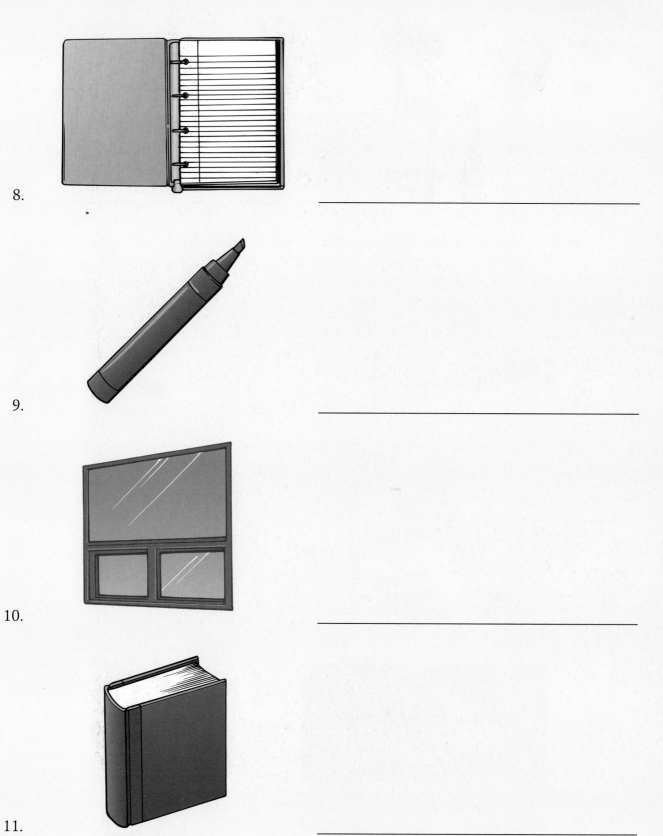

8. _____

9. _____

10. _____

11. _____

12. _____

13. _____

14. _____

15. _____

D Ergänze die Sätze! *(Complete the sentences.)*

1. _____ ist das?

2. Das ist _____ Kuli.

3. Das ist _____ Uhr.

4. Das ist _____ Heft.

E **Do what your teacher commands.**

F Ergänze die Sätze auf Deutsch, bitte! *(Complete the sentences in German, please.)*

1. _____ deutsch! (Speak)

2. _____ das auf Deutsch! (Say)

3. _____ zu! (Listen)

4. _____ den Computer _____! (Turn off)

5. _____ das Buch _____! (Open)

G Ergänze die Sätze auf Deutsch, bitte! *(Complete the sentences in German, please.)*

1. Nimm _____ heraus!

2. Wiederhole die _____!

3. Mach das _____ zu!

4. Zeichne ein _____!

5. Schalte den _____ an!

6. Schreib mit *(with)* einem _____!

7. Beantworte die _____!

H Schreib einen Befehl zu jeder Abbildung auf Deutsch! *(Write a command in German for each illustration.)*

1. _____

2.  _____

3.  _____

4.  _____

5.  _____

Die Klasse und Imperative

I Which objects go together? Match each noun in column *A* with a related noun in column *B*.

A	B
1. _____ eine Maus	A. eine Wand
2. _____ ein Schreibtisch	B. ein Bildschirm
3. _____ ein Filzstift	C. ein Heft
4. _____ ein Blatt Papier	D. eine Tafel
5. _____ ein Bild	E. ein Stuhl

J **Zum Sprechen.** Point to a classroom object, such as a ruler and ask, *"Ist das ein Lineal?"* Your speaking partner should answer, *"Ja, das ist ein Lineal."* Point to a map and ask, *"Ist das ein Bleistift?"* Your partner should answer, *"Nein, das ist eine Landkarte."* Find ten items to discuss.

K Word associations. You and your speaking partner should each make a list of five words from the classroom commands. Ask each other to say anything related to that word.

> Beispiele: A: *die Hand*
> B: *Heb!*
> and
> B: *Sag das*
> A: *auf Deutsch!*

L **Du bist dran!** Walk around your classroom with a partner, pointing to ten different objects. Ask your partner, *"Was ist das?"* If he/she answers incorrectly, switch roles. Now it is his/her turn to ask you the name of each item. Keep going until all ten objects have been correctly identified.

Sprichwort

Was Hänschen nicht lernt, lernt Hans nimmermehr.
You can't teach an old dog new tricks.

Lebendige Sprache

1 **Englisch im Beruf!**
Werden Sie fit
mit einem Kompaktkurs
Business-Englisch.
SPRACHEN & BILDUNG 🕿
Ludwigsburg, Alleenstraße 4, Tel. 90 54 56

2
Spanisch
www.i-l-e.de
Info: Tel. 0 71 42/98 01 30

3
**PLS Sprachen-
schule Mehler**
Englisch, Spanisch, Französisch,
Italienisch, Chinesisch,
Deutsch als Fremdsprache;
Intensivkurse
Solitudestr. 44 · 71638 Ludwigsburg
Tel. **(0 71 41) 92 04 46**
E-Mail: plsmehler@aol.com

4
Sprachkurse
Englisch, Französisch, Spanisch
Italienisch, Deutsch, Russisch
im Einzelunterricht oder in kleinen Gruppen
Seniorenkurse
SPRACHEN & BILDUNG
Ludwigsburg, Alleenstraße 4, Tel. 90 54 56

5 **Brush up your English**
Engländerin bietet
Konversation Englisch.
Tel. 01 79-6 57 30 86

6 **Boris Prévot**
Musikschule
Leonberger Straße 48
71638 Ludwigsburg
Mo.–Mi. 14.00–19.00 Uhr
Tel.: (0 71 41) 92 72 94
Do.–Fr. 8.00–19.00 Uhr
Tel. (0 71 91) 2 25 30
**Keybord-, Orgel-,
Klavier- u. Akkordeon-
Unterricht**
Einzel- u. Gruppenunterricht
Für Schüler von 7–99 Jahren
2 kostenlose Probestunden

MEIN STUNDENPLAN

ZEIT	MONTAG	DIENSTAG	MITTWOCH	DONNERSTAG	FREITAG
7.45–8.30	Englisch	Sport	Gemeinschaftskunde	Biologie	Mathematik
8.35–9.20	Mathematik	Sport	Religion	Griechisch	Englisch
9.20–9.35	Große Pause	Große Pause	Große Pause	Große Pause	Große Pause
9.35–10.20	Griechisch	Geschichte	Griechisch	Mathematik	Gemeinschaftskunde
10.25–11.10	Chemie	Mathematik	Englisch	Englisch	Geschichte
11.10–11.20	Pause	Pause	Pause	Pause	Pause
11.20–12.05	Physik	Latein	Latein	Deutsch	Religion
12.10–12.55	Deutsch	Deutsch	Chor	Chemie	Latein
14.20–15.05		Biologie	Kunst		
15.10–15.55		Griechisch	Musik		

M Look at the ads and match each one with its appropriate description.

1. _____
2. _____
3. _____
4. _____
5. _____
6. _____

A. Private lessons in Chinese can be taken here.

B. A lady from England offers to improve your conversational English.

C. Professionals who want to improve their English skills in the business world can sign up for this course.

D. Students who want to learn how to play a musical instrument can contact this school.

E. You can sign up for Spanish classes either on their website or by calling.

F. Courses for senior citizens are offered.

N Review this tenth grade schedule and then answer the questions. Although you don't know most of these words, you can figure out many of them. To get you started, here are some new words that you may not be able to figure out: *Große Pause* long recess, *Geschichte* history, *Gemeinschaftskunde* social studies, *Kunst* art.

1. How long is each class period?

   _____

2. How many foreign languages does this student study and what are they?

   _____

3. When do students go home on Fridays?

   _____

4. How many times per week do students have math?

   _____

5. On which day and at what time do students have choir?

   _____

6. How much time is there between classes?

   _____

Symtalk

O **Ergänze die richtigen Wörter auf Deutsch.** *(In the space, write the correct word in German.)*

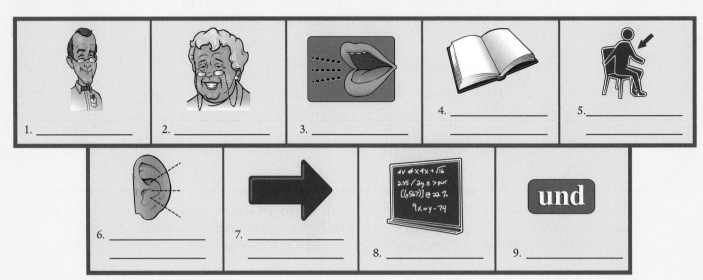

1. _____
2. _____
3. _____
4. _____
5. _____
6. _____
7. _____
8. _____
9. _____

P **Sag die Sätze! Dann schreib sie auf Deutsch!** *(Say the sentences, then write them in German.)*

1. _____

2. _____

3. _____

4. _____

_____

Q **Beschreibe jede Szene! Auf Deutsch, bitte!** *(In German, write a description of each scene.)*

1.

_____

_____

_____

_____

2.

_____

_____

_____

_____

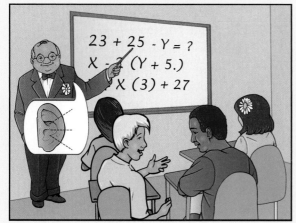

3.

_____

_____

_____

_____

Kreuzworträtsel

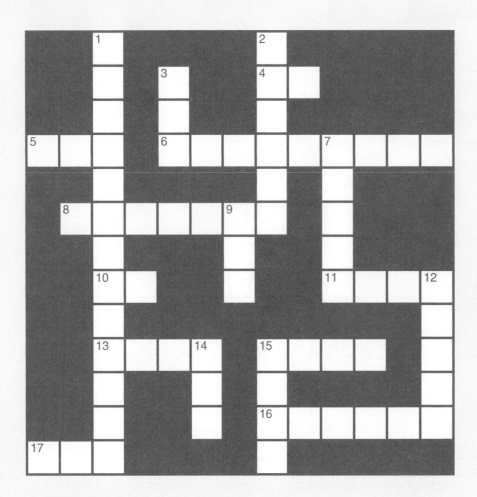

Waagerecht

4. *Schalte den Computer* ____! (Turn the computer on.)
5. what
6. writing instrument
8. where light comes in
10. *Mach das Buch* ____! (Close.)
11. Read.
13. gadget used to point at something
15. what is written, printed, bound, and read
16. makes straight lines
17. tells you the time

Senkrecht

1. place of instruction
2. *ein Blatt* ____
3. ____ *die Hand!*
7. place to write
9. *Das ist* ____ *Kuli.*
12. place to sit
14. Say.
15. wall decoration

UNIT 3

Die Zahlen

Numbers

Vokabeln

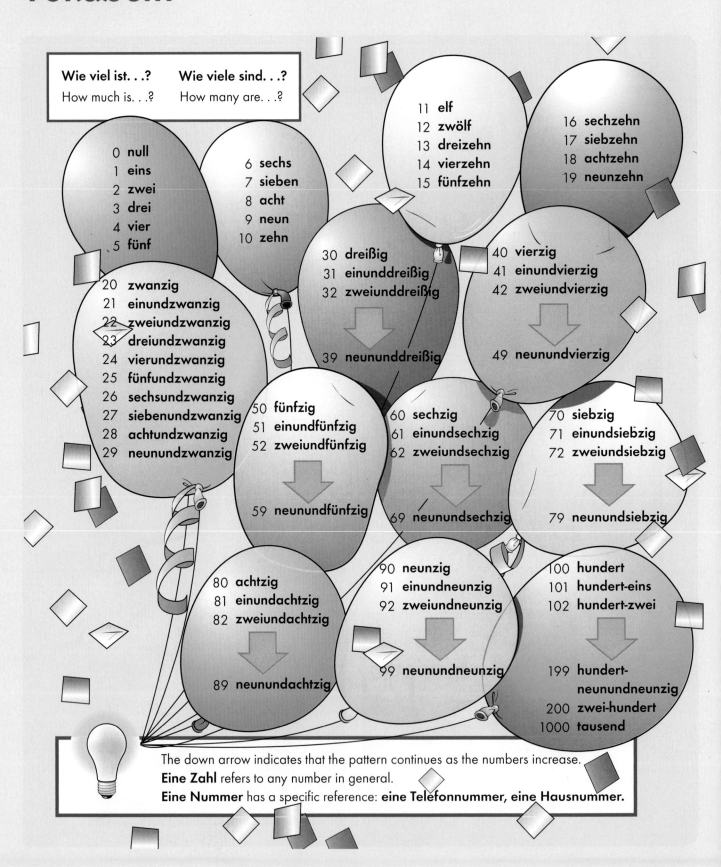

0 null
1 eins
2 zwei
3 drei
4 vier
5 fünf

6 sechs
7 sieben
8 acht
9 neun
10 zehn

11 elf
12 zwölf
13 dreizehn
14 vierzehn
15 fünfzehn

16 sechzehn
17 siebzehn
18 achtzehn
19 neunzehn

20 zwanzig
21 einundzwanzig
22 zweiundzwanzig
23 dreiundzwanzig
24 vierundzwanzig
25 fünfundzwanzig
26 sechsundzwanzig
27 siebenundzwanzig
28 achtundzwanzig
29 neunundzwanzig

30 dreißig
31 einunddreißig
32 zweiunddreißig

39 neununddreißig

40 vierzig
41 einundvierzig
42 zweiundvierzig

49 neunundvierzig

50 fünfzig
51 einundfünfzig
52 zweiundfünfzig

59 neunundfünfzig

60 sechzig
61 einundsechzig
62 zweiundsechzig

69 neunundsechzig

70 siebzig
71 einundsiebzig
72 zweiundsiebzig

79 neunundsiebzig

80 achtzig
81 einundachtzig
82 zweiundachtzig

89 neunundachtzig

90 neunzig
91 einundneunzig
92 zweiundneunzig

99 neunundneunzig

100 hundert
101 hundert-eins
102 hundert-zwei

199 hundert-neunundneunzig
200 zwei-hundert
1000 tausend

The down arrow indicates that the pattern continues as the numbers increase.
Eine Zahl refers to any number in general.
Eine Nummer has a specific reference: **eine Telefonnummer, eine Hausnummer.**

Extra Vokabeln

Wie viel?
How much?

Wie viele?
How many?

es gibt
there is, there are

Gibt es. . .?
Is there/Are there. . .?

Wie viel kostet das Buch?
How much does the book cost?

Das Buch kostet € 15.
The book costs fifteen euros.

Wie viele Hefte gibt es?
How many notebooks are there?

Es gibt zwölf Hefte.
There are twelve notebooks.

Wie viel ist zwei und eins?
How much is two and one?

Wie viel macht das?
How much does that make?

Das macht drei.
That makes three.

kosten
to cost

es kostet
it costs

sie kosten
they cost

$+$ = *und* $\times$ = *mal* $-$ = *weniger* $\div$ = *geteilt durch*

- The currency of Germany is the euro *(der Euro)*. The plural form is the same (die *Euro*). One cent is *ein Cent*. The euro contains *100 Cent*.
- *Euros* and *cents* are separated by a comma. *Die CD kostet € 18,50.*

50 cents

20 cents

10 euros

Übungen

A After you have studied the numbers and practiced saying them, try to write the numbers from memory. *Auf Deutsch, bitte.*

1 _____   6 _____

2 _____   7 _____

3 _____   8 _____

4 _____   9 _____

5 _____   10 _____

B Rate yourself. How did you do? Circle your evaluation.

1. very well *(sehr gut)* _____   2. fairly well *(ganz gut)* _____   3. poorly *(schlecht)* _____

C Practice again. Identify the words by making the corresponding Arabic numerals.

> Beispiel: zwei __2__

1. fünf _____
2. acht _____

3. eins _____
4. neun _____

5. sieben _____

D Schreib das deutsche Wort für jede Zahl! *(Write the German word for each number.)*

1. (3) _____
2. (4) _____

3. (6) _____
4. (10) _____

E Tell whether each equation indicates addition, subtraction, multiplication, or division.

1. Vierzehn geteilt durch sieben ist zwei. _____

2. Zwei und zehn ist zwölf. _____

3. Acht mal drei ist vierundzwanzig. _____

4. Neunzehn weniger dreizehn ist sechs. _____

F Try once more to write out the German words for numbers. *Auf Deutsch, bitte.*

8 _____
3 _____
10 _____
1 _____
9 _____

2 _____
5 _____
4 _____
7 _____
6 _____

G Wie viele Objekte gibt es hier? *(How many objects are pictured? Write out the German numbers. Do not use numerals!)*

1. _____

2. 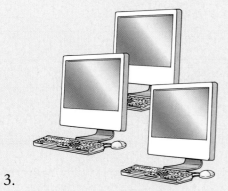 _____

3. _____

4. _____

5.  _____

H **Wie viele Objekte gibt es zusammen?** *(How many objects are there altogether?)* _____

Now, write this sum in German.

_____

I **Schreib die Antworten auf Deutsch!** *(Write the answers in German).*

> **Beispiel:** 6 − 4 = __zwei__

1. $12 \times 4 =$ _____
2. $30 - 10 =$ _____
3. $8 - 6 =$ _____
4. $12 + 18 =$ _____
5. $100 \div 2 =$ _____
6. $60 + 10 =$ _____
7. $30 - 15 =$ _____
8. $80 \div 2 =$ _____
9. $10 \times 10 =$ _____
10. $15 + 4 =$ _____

J **Your teacher will say ten numbers in German. Write the corresponding Arabic numerals.**

> **Beispiel:** Teacher says: neunzehn
> You write: _____19_____

1. _____ 4. _____ 7. _____ 9. _____

2. _____ 5. _____ 8. _____ 10. _____

3. _____ 6. _____

K **How many interior angles are there in each design? Circle the number.**

1.   vier   zehn
    acht   drei

3.   sieben   fünf
    sechs   elf

2.   fünf   drei
    vier   sieben

4.   elf   acht
    neun   fünf

L Lies den Absatz! Dann wähle die richtigen Antworten! *(Read the paragraph. Then choose the correct answers.)*

> Im Klassenzimmer gibt es viele Objekte. Es gibt achtundzwanzig Stühle, vier Fenster, neunzehn Hefte, sechs Wischer, und eine Landkarte. Ein Stuhl kostet fünfundsiebzig Euro. Ein Wischer kostet einen Euro und eine Landkarte kostet achtzig Euro.

1. **Im Klassenzimmer gibt es ___ Objekte.**
   A. wenige
   B. viele
   C. acht
   D. zehn

2. **Es gibt insgesamt *(totally)* ___ Objekte.**
   A. einundvierzig
   B. achtundfünfzig
   C. zweiundzwanzig
   D. neunzig

3. **Wie viel kostet ein Stuhl?**
   A. € 75
   B. € 57
   C. € 37
   D. € 73

4. **Wie viele Hefte gibt es?**
   A. 91
   B. 25
   C. 19
   D. 30

5. **Wie viele Fenster gibt es?**
   A. 13
   B. 8
   C. 6
   D. 4

M Zum Sprechen. Find out about prices. With your speaking partner select six objects in the classroom. You ask about the first three and ask how much each one costs. Then your partner will ask you about the remaining three items and you will answer.

> Beispiel: A: Wie viel kostet der Kuli?
> B: Der Kuli kostet zwei Euro.

N Du bist dran! With a classmate, discover how many things are in your classroom. Look for these items: *Bücher* (books), *Fenster* (windows), *Hefte* (notebooks), *Kulis* (pens), *Computer*, and *Schreibtische* (desks). After you have counted carefully, announce your findings to the class. How many books are there? At the end add all the items to find out the total number of things you have. Write all numbers on your classroom board.

> Beispiel: A: *Wie viele Bücher gibt es?* (How many books are there?)
> B: *Es gibt zwanzig Bücher.* (There are twenty books.)

Lebendige Sprache

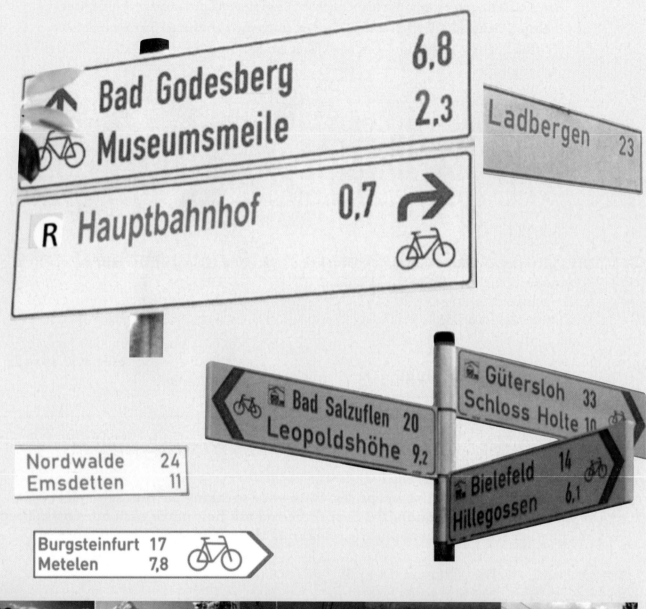

Bad Godesberg 6,8
Museumsmeile 2,3

Ladbergen 23

R Hauptbahnhof 0,7

Bad Salzuflen 20
Leopoldshöhe 9,2

Gütersloh 33
Schloss Holte 10

Bielefeld 14
Hillegossen 6,1

Nordwalde 24
Emsdetten 11

Burgsteinfurt 17
Metelen 7,8

O Throughout German-speaking countries you'll see signs indicating distances to various towns and other specific places. Write out the number of kilometers in German for the distances indicated for each place. Notice that Germans use a comma (versus a decimal point) for indicating fractions. Whenever there is a fraction or comma, write *Komma*.

> **Beispiel:** *Hauptbahnhof 0,7 = null, Komma, sieben*

1. Bad Salzuflen: _____
2. Metelen: _____
3. Bad Godesberg: _____
4. Gütersloh: _____
5. Norwalde: _____
6. Hillegossen: _____
7. Museumsmeile: _____
8. Ladbergen: _____
9. Burgsteinfurt: _____
10. Leopoldshöhe: _____

P The town of Garmisch-Partenkirchen in southern Germany is a popular ski area. Look at the address and write out the following numbers in German.

1. Fax number: _____
   _____
2. Street number: _____
3. Zip code: _____
4. Phone number: _____
   _____

Sprichwort

Jede Münze hat zwei Seiten.
There are two sides to every story.

Symtalk

Q **Ergänze die richtigen Wörter auf Deutsch!** *(In the space, write the correct word in German.)*

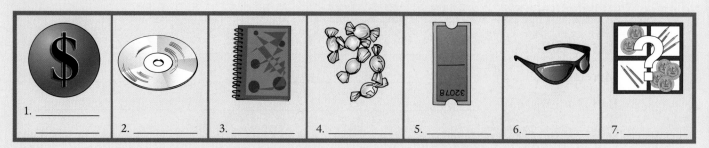

1. _____ 2. _____ 3. _____ 4. _____ 5. _____ 6. _____ 7. _____

R **Sag die Sätze! Dann schreib sie auf Deutsch!** *(Say the sentences, then write them in German.)*

1. _____

2. _____

3. _____

4. _____

S **Wie viel kostet jeder Gegenstand? Schreib es auf Deutsch, bitte!** *(How much does each object cost? Write in German, please.)*

€ **der Euro   die Euro**

1.

_____   _____

2.

_____   _____

3.

_____   _____

4.

_____   _____

Kreuzworträtsel

Waagerecht

1. 70 + 30
7. currency of Germany
8. between *zehn* and *zwölf*
11. _____ *viel?*
12. numbers
13. the number of items in a pair
14. number of days in a week
15. 30 × 2

Senkrecht

2. word that indicates addition
3. dozen plus one
4. number of seasons
5. multiplied by
6. *Wie viel _____ das Buch?*
9. ½ of *hundert*
10. number after *neununddreißig*
11. word that indicates subtraction
12. *vier mal fünf*

UNIT 4

Die Geografie

Geography

Vokabeln

Die Geografie

Deutschland (Germany)

As a member of the European Union, Germany is committed to a friendly economic alliance with 27 other nations. The "Euro" is the currency used in many of these nations.

Berlin, the capital of Germany, is a major industrial, educational and cultural center. The landmark of the city is the Brandenburg Gate, a Greek-styled structure built in 1791. Berlin's most famous museum, the *Pergamon*, houses archeological exhibits from ancient Greece. A newer landmark is the glass dome of the *Reichstag*, the Parliament building of the German government. Here visitors can walk up a ramp into the dome and enjoy a panoramic view of the entire city.

There are many parks and lakes in the Berlin area for picnics and water sports. Visitors often go to the *Zoologischer Garten* (zoo) and to the 18th century palace of *Charlottenburg*. Celebrities attend the annual Berlin Film Festival at which the best films are awarded the Golden Bear trophy. (The name *Berlin* refers to the bear, a symbol of the city.)

Palmengarten in Frankfurt

Frankfurt am Main is a banking city known as the financial heart of the nation. The author Johann Wolfgang von Goethe was born here. Visitors enjoy the zoo and the *Palmengarten*, a botanical garden with tropical plants. The city hosts an annual book fair for international booksellers. The *Frankfurter Flughafen* is Germany's largest airport. Millions of travelers pass through this international airport. (Frankfurt's name comes from the word *furt*, which is a ford or narrow part of the river. The Frankish people once lived at this site.)

Köln (or Cologne) is a major city located on the *Rhein* (Rhine) River. The huge Gothic Cathedral, started in 1248 and completed in 1880, gives Köln its nickname, the Cathedral City. It is known generally as a city of art galleries and commercial trade fairs. Its most famous product is called *Echt Kölnisch Wasser 4711*, a light cologne originally created over 200 years ago. Every year the city celebrates the pre-Lenten festival of Carnival with elaborate parades and floats. Over one million people visit the city to attend this fun-filled event. (The name *Köln* is derived from the Latin word *colonia*, or colony, because the city was founded by the Romans in 50 A.D.)

Hamburg is the largest seaport of Germany and a major industrial center. It lies where the Elbe River empties into the North Sea. Hagenbeck's Animal Park is here, as well as lakes and parks for jogging and biking. Hamburg is in the Guinness Book of Records as the European city with the largest number of bridges. It is called the "Venice of the

North." Near the city is *Heide-Park Soltau,* a gigantic amusement park with roller coasters, water slides, white water rapids, and stage shows. (The name *Hamburg* comes from a very old fort called the Hammaburg or Hamma Castle.)

München (or Munich) is a major industrial and cultural center. It is the site of automobile and aircraft production, higher education, scientific research, and the movie industry. The local people are proud of their traditions and cultural heritage. The *Nymphenburg* palace is one of the city's most impressive buildings. The *Oktoberfest,* which attracts hundreds of tourists each year, is the largest folk festival in the world. Residents and visitors to Munich can enjoy the Olympic Park facilities all year long. They can also tour the film studio *Bavaria Filmstadt* to see the settings for television shows. Soccer fans enjoy a state-of-the-art stadium built for the 2006 World Cup games. (*München* started as a monastery, that is, a residence for monks. The city's name comes from the word *Mönch,* or monk, the symbol of the city.)

Leipzig

Der Zwinger in Dresden

Leipzig has a long history as a trade and business center. Today it is a fast-growing industrial city. It will soon be the major center for air freight transportation in Europe. It is also a center for shows and trade fairs *(Messen).* As such, it is often called the City of Fairs, or *Messestadt.* A double "M" is a symbol of the city. Leipzig is also the home of the *Gewandhausorchester* and the St. Thomas Boys' Choir. Young people interested in seeing and learning about professional theater enjoy theatrical performances in the *Theater der Jungen Welt.* The *Belantis* theme park near the city offers exciting adventures for the entire family.

Dresden is called the "Florence of the North" because of its long association with art and culture. One of its historic buildings is a baroque palace called the *Zwinger.* It houses valuable art collections. Located on the Elbe River, the city is also a manufacturing and industrial center. Many people know this city as the home of a holiday fruit bread, the *Dresdner Stollen.* The nearby town of Meissen still manufactures porcelain, creating the world famous Dresden china. (*Dresden blue* is a shade made famous by the manufacturing company.)

Schweiz (Switzerland)

Bern is the capital of the nation. It is located on the Aare River. Like Berlin in Germany, the name *Bern* is associated with bears. The city has an annual international jazz festival.

Genf (or Geneva) is an international conference center and the site of several agencies of the United Nations. Located on *Genfer See* (Lake Geneva), the small city serves as a second home to many international film stars and celebrities. The entrance to the harbor is marked by a gigantic water spray.

Zürich is a major banking center. Situated on *Zürichsee* (Lake Zurich), this city attracts business people as well as sightseers and boaters.

Switzerland has picturesque alpine resort areas such as the city of *Luzern* (or Lucerne) and ski centers such as Gstaad and St. Moritz. The Matterhorn is the country's tallest mountain.

Zürich

Österreich (Austria)

Wien (or Vienna) is the capital and largest city of Austria. It is the headquarters of major industries and the second European home of the United Nations. Situated on the *Donau* (Danube River), it is also a busy port for international cargo. Historically known as a city of music, Wien has always appreciated the musicians, composers and singers who have lived or performed there. It is the home of the Vienna Boys' Choir and the Spanish Riding School, the latter known for trained white Lippizan stallions.

Salzburg, the birthplace of the composer Wolfgang Amadeus Mozart, is a city noted for both its beautiful alpine setting as well as the Salzburg Music Festival. The filming of the motion picture *Sound of Music* took place in Salzburg. (The city derives its name from a salt mine and a castle.)

Salzburg

Die Elbe

Important Rivers

The ***Donau*** (or Danube), starts in southwestern Germany, flows east and south, and empties into the Black Sea. It is a major transportation route.

The ***Rhein*** (or Rhine) originates in Switzerland, flows through Germany, and serves as a natural border with France and then goes north and west through the Netherlands, finally reaching the North Sea. It also is a major commercial and scenic river. The city of Köln is located on this river.

The ***Elbe River*** is a major commercial river originating in the Czech Republic and flowing northwest into the North Sea. The cities of Dresden and Hamburg are both situated on this river.

The ***Main River*** flows west and joins the Rhine River. Although short, it provides a needed waterway for the central area of the country. The city of Frankfurt am Main is located on this river.

Important Facts

- Germany has an extensive system of canals which connect many rivers and parts of the country. The canals help with the transportation of imported and exported products.

- *Nordsee* stands for North Sea, but *Ostsee* (literally, East Sea) is called the Baltic Sea.

- The *Bodensee* is called Lake Constance.

- The principality of Liechtenstein, located between Austria and Switzerland, is a highly industrialized modern nation. It uses the Swiss franc for currency.

Übungen

A **Write the letter of each city on the map next to its name below.**

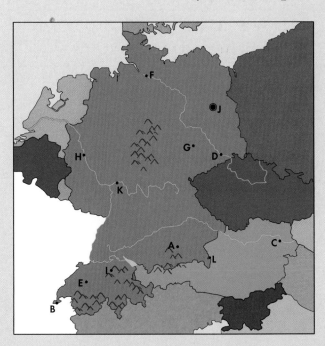

1. _____ Leipzig
2. _____ Zürich
3. _____ Hamburg
4. _____ Frankfurt am Main
5. _____ Berlin
6. _____ Dresden
7. _____ Köln
8. _____ Wien
9. _____ Bern
10. _____ München
11. _____ Salzburg
12. _____ Genf

B **Identify the cities described in the information below.**

1. home of the Spanish Riding school _____
2. site of the annual *Oktoberfest* _____
3. city noted for a pleasant fragrance _____
4. symbol is the double M _____
5. site of the Brandenburg Gate _____
6. major seaport with parks and lakes _____
7. city known for art and porcelain _____
8. city noted for a music festival _____
9. Swiss banking center _____
10. birthplace of writer J. W. von Goethe _____
11. city that sponsors a jazz festival _____
12. city with a book fair every year _____

C Study the map carefully. Then find the following items.

1. the river that divides Germany from France

_____

2. the river that flows eastward through Austria

_____

3. the lake that borders on three countries

_____

4. the large middle European mountain range

_____

5. the small country between Austria and Switzerland

_____

Die Alpen in Österreich

Winter in der Schweiz

Match Column *A* with Column *B*.

	A		B
1. _____	Frankfurt am Main	A.	City in northern Switzerland
2. _____	München	B.	City that hosts a Carnival parade
3. _____	Leipzig	C.	Place where salt was mined
4. _____	Wien	D.	Home of a botanical garden
5. _____	Zürich	E.	Home of St. Thomas Boys' Choir
6. _____	Hamburg	F.	Home of the *Charlottenburg* palace
7. _____	Salzburg	G.	Home of the *Nymphenburg* palace
8. _____	Köln	H.	"Florence of the North"
9. _____	Berlin	I.	"Venice of the North"
10. _____	Dresden	J.	Capital of Austria

E **Schreib den Namen der Stadt, die zur jeder Abbildung passt!** *(Name the city associated with each illustration.)*

1.  _____

2.  _____

3. _____

4. _____

5. _____

F **Wähle die richtige Antwort!** *(Choose the correct answer.)*

1. *Wien* is the capital city of ___.
   A. Germany
   B. Liechtenstein
   C. Switzerland
   D. Austria

2. *Bodensee* is the name of a ___.
   A. lake
   B. city
   C. river
   D. sea

3. *München* is a city in the ___ of Germany.
   A. south
   B. east
   C. north
   D. west

4. *Salzburg* lies to the ___ of *Wien*.
   A. north
   B. south
   C. west
   D. east

5. *Frankfurt* lies on the ____ River.
   A. Elbe
   B. Main
   C. Rhein
   D. Donau

8. *Leipzig* is a ____.
   A. river
   B. country
   C. city
   D. lake

6. *Berlin* is located ____ of Leipzig.
   A. west
   B. south
   C. east
   D. north

9. The *Alpen* form a ____.
   A. country
   B. mountain range
   C. river
   D. lake

7. Poland lies to the ____ of Germany.
   A. east
   B. north
   C. west
   D. south

10. In Germany, the lowlands are in the ____.
    A. south
    B. west
    C. north
    D. east

G **Write in each blank space the answer that makes each statement geographically correct.**

Located in northern Europe, Germany has a variety of geographical features. It has two

seacoasts, one on the *Nordsee,* or (1) _____, and the other on the

Ostsee, or (2) _____. Crossed by canals and dotted with many

small lakes, the northern lowlands cover about one-third of the country. The *Bodensee,*

located in the southern part of Germany, borders on Germany, Switzerland and

(3) _____.

Germany has many neighbors. Far to the north is (4) _____.

Continuing to the right on the east are (5) _____ and

(6) _____. On its southern border are (7) _____ and

(8) _____. On its western side are (9) _____,

(10) _____, (11) _____, and

(12) _____.

The huge Alpine mountain range has magnificent scenery, including glaciers and mountain

lakes. However, there is always the possibility of avalanches, especially in the spring. Mountain

climbing and skiing are popular pastimes in the Alpine countries. Two well-known ski resorts

are (13) _____ and (14) _____.

H Imagine that you are a German official trying to convince a group of American business people to establish companies in Germany. List five cities to which you would take the group and explain why you selected these cities.

_____
_____
_____
_____
_____
_____
_____
_____
_____
_____

I Imagine that you must plan an itinerary (list of sightseeing places) for a group of tourists who would like to see some cultural sites in Germany, Austria, or Switzerland. (Cultural sites are those places which have to do with history, music, art or theater.) List five places you would recommend and explain why you selected these cities.

_____
_____
_____
_____
_____
_____
_____
_____
_____
_____

J Natascha and Nils are ready to travel! Trace their vacation route to find out where they will be spending the summer. Name their destination in the space provided.

Places they'll visit:

_____
_____
_____
_____
_____
_____

Messestadt

Hameln
Frankfurt/Main
Luzern
Potsdam
Passau
Landau/Isar
Kiel
Celle
Halle
Ulm
Würzburg
Innsbruck
Linz
Göttingen
Gießen
Bremen
Schwerin
Dortmund
Rostock
Hannover
Lübeck
Rothenburg/Tauber

Their destination is:

_____

K **Du bist dran!** Play travel agency! Pretend that you are going on a trip to a German-speaking country. Ask for recommendations of places to visit. Your friend will play the part of the travel agent and make several suggestions. You might also like to say hello, and later, say thank you and good-bye in German!

Lebendige Sprache

Die Geografie

L **Look at the map and then write the answers in the blank spaces provided. Be sure to give the German names for all the countries and cities. The various distances are provided from the city of Braunschweig.**

Germany has (1.) _____ neighboring countries. The country immediately to the north of Germany is called (2.) _____. There are two seas located to the northwest and northeast of Germany. The sea located to the northwest is called in (write in German) (3.) _____ and to the northeast is called (4.) _____. The most northern German city indicated is (5.) _____. The city of Dresden is located in the (list direction) (6.) _____ of the country. When heading directly east of Berlin, you would end up in the country of (7.) _____.

The closest city from Braunschweig is (8.) _____, about (9.) _____ kilometers away. Prag is the capital of the (10.) _____. The farthest city from Braunschweig as shown on the map is the Austrian city (11.) _____. The nearest city to Frankfurt shown on the map is (12.) _____. The distance from Stuttgart to Braunschweig is (13.) _____ km. A Belgium city shown is called (14.) _____. The official German name for Holland is (15.) die _____. Two cities in Switzerland shown are (16.) _____ and (17.) _____. The second Swiss city is closer to (18.) _____. Its distance is 720 (19.)_____.

Sprichwort

Andere Länder, andere Sitten.

When in Rome, do as the Romans do.

Symtalk

M Ergänze die richtigen Wörter auf Deutsch! *(In the space, write the correct word in German.)*

1. _____

2. _____

3. _____

4. _____

5. _____

N Sag die Sätze! Dann schreib sie auf Deutsch! *(Say the sentences, then write them in German.)*

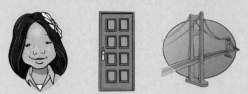

1. _____

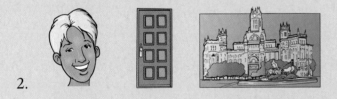

2. _____

3. _____

4. _____

O Mit einem Klassenkameraden, stell die Frage oder gib die Antwort! *(With a partner, ask the question or give the answer. Then, write the dialogue.)*

1.   _____

_____

2.    _____

_____

3.    _____

_____

4.   _____

_____

5.

_____

Kreuzworträtsel

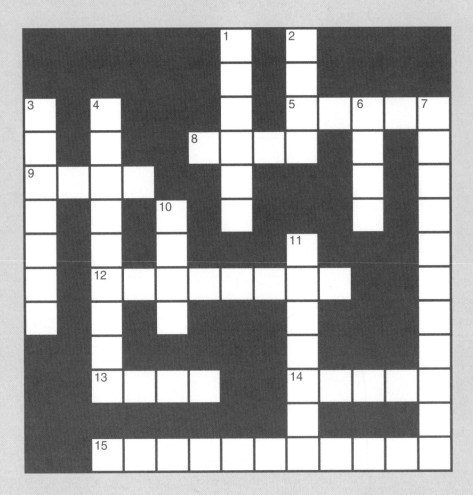

Waagerecht

5. river that starts in Switzerland
8. European home of the United Nations
9. river that flows westward into the Rhine River
12. birthplace of the composer Mozart
13. city at edge of Lake Geneva (German spelling)
14. the Danube River (German spelling)
15. name of the landmark gate in Berlin

Senkrecht

1. banking center of Switzerland
2. site of a jazz festival
3. "Venice of the North"
4. government building with a new glass dome
6. river that starts in the Czech Republic
7. palace in Munich
10. Cathedral City
11. "Florence of the North"

UNIT 5

Das Haus

House

Vokabeln

KATJA:	**Wo wohnst du?**	Where do you live?
JULIA:	**Ich wohne in einem Haus in Köln.**	I live in a house in Köln.
MICHAEL:	**Wo ist der Garten?**	Where is the garden?
JOHANN:	**Der Garten ist da drüben.**	The garden is over there.
MAHMOOD:	**Wo ist die Garage?**	Where is the garage?
HALIMA:	**Sie ist hinter dem Garten.**	It's behind the garden.
SOPHIE:	**Wie viele Zimmer gibt es in deinem Haus?**	How many rooms are there in your house?
LISBETH:	**Es gibt acht Zimmer.**	There are eight rooms.

- Each German noun belongs to one of three gender categories: masculine, feminine, and neuter. Each category has its own word for *the*:

    der (in front of a masculine singular noun): **der Garten**

    die (in front of a feminine singular noun): **die Garage**

    das (in front of a neuter singular noun): **das Haus**
- If the noun is plural, then the definite article *the* is **die** (pronounced DEE): **die Zimmer** (the rooms)
- The word **Garten** can mean yard, as well.

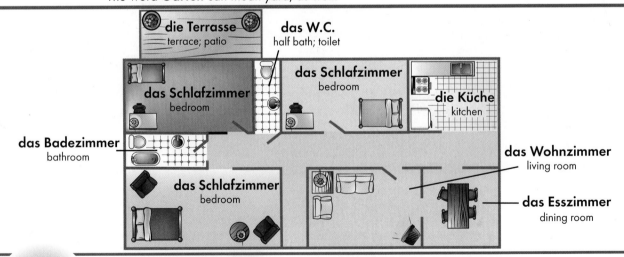

- Hospitality is part of German culture. Being gracious to one's guests includes making them feel at home.
- **Das Zimmer** refers to a room in a house.

Extra Vokabeln

die Villa

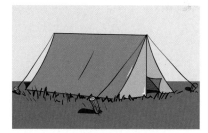

die Wohnung
die Eigentumswohnung

das Einfamilienhaus

die Hütte

das Mietshaus

das Zelt

Übungen

A **Schreib das deutsche Wort für jedes Zimmer!** *(Write the German word for each room.)*

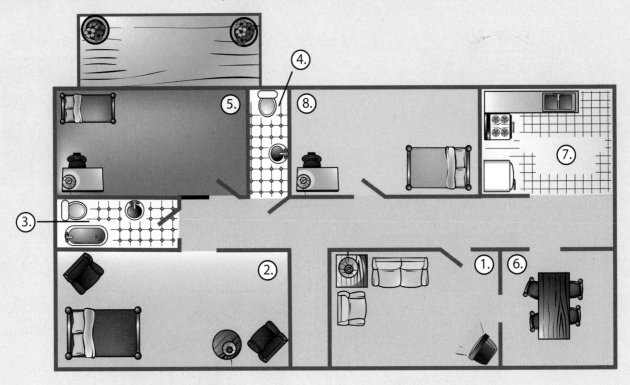

1. _____   5. _____

2. _____   6. _____

3. _____   7. _____

4. _____   8. _____

B **Ergänze die Sätze!** *(Complete the sentences in German with the names of the house-related vocabulary.)*

1. Ich koche *(cook)* in der _____.

2. Ich schlafe *(sleep)* in dem _____.

3. Ich esse *(eat)* in dem _____.

4. Ich bade *(bathe)* in dem _____.

5. Ich spiele *(play)* in dem _____.

6. Ich entspanne mich *(relax)* in dem _____.

   oder *(or)* auf der _____.

C

Wähle das richtige Zimmer! *(Choose the correct English room.)*

1. Esszimmer: *dining room*   *kitchen*   *living room*
2. Küche: *bedroom*   *living room*   *kitchen*
3. Schlafzimmer: *dining room*   *bedroom*   *bathroom*
4. Badezimmer: *living room*   *bathroom*   *bedroom*
5. Wohnzimmer   *bathroom*   *kitchen*   *living room*

D

In which room would you find a . . . *(Auf Deutsch, bitte.)*

1. dining table? _____
2. refrigerator? _____
3. alarm clock? _____
4. piano? _____
5. shower? _____
6. stove? _____
7. sofa? _____
8. tablecloth? _____
9. toilet? _____
10. dresser? _____

E

Identify each description with the appropriate German word.

1. place to sleep at a camp site _____
2. renter's residence in a building _____
3. homeowner's residence _____
4. millionaire's residence _____
5. place to park an automobile _____

F

Schreib die Wörter richtig! *(Unscramble the words.)*

1. ELTZ _____
2. MEIMZR _____
3. ÜKECH _____
4. ASHU _____
5. TRAGEN _____

G **Lies den Absatz! Ergänze die Sätze richtig.** *(Read the paragraph. Then, choose the correct words to complete each sentence.)*

Hier ist mein Haus. Es ist *schön*. Meine Familie wohnt hier. Ich liebe meine Familie und mein Haus. Das Haus *hat* sieben Zimmer. Es gibt viele *Blumen* im Garten Die Terrasse ist hinter dem Haus.

HAUS   FAMILIE

schön beautiful   **hat** has   **Blumen** flowers

1. Meine Familie wohnt ___.
   A. Zimmer
   B. in einem Haus
   C. Terrasse
   D. Garten

2. Mein Haus ist ___.
   A. neu
   B. alt
   C. schön
   D. klein

3. Mein Haus hat ___ Zimmer.
   A. fünf
   B. sechs
   C. sieben
   D. acht

4. Die Terrasse ist hinter dem ___.
   A. Haus
   B. Familie
   C. Zimmer
   D. Garten

H Zum Sprechen. **Point to a picture of a room in a house. Ask your speaking partner in German: "Is that a bedroom?" He/she should answer: "No, that's a kitchen." or "Yes, that's a bedroom." Take turns asking and answering about all the rooms in the house.**

I Zum Sprechen. **Point to one of the types of residences shown in your book. As you do this, ask your classmate where an imaginary student lives. He/she should answer appropriately.**

> Beispiel: A: *(points to an apartment)* Wo wohnt Tim?
> B: Tim wohnt in einer Wohnung.

J Du bist dran! **Find out where people live. With your partner make a list of 5 famous people. Then ask your classmate in German: *Wo wohnt...?* adding the name of a famous person. Your classmate should answer by writing down the city or country in his/her notebook.**

Sprichwort

Eigener Herd ist Goldes wert.

There's no place like home.

Lebendige Sprache

A

Wohnen in gewachsenem Gebiet!
Bietigheim-Bissingen € 389.000,–
Freistehendes Einfamilienwohnhaus, groß-
zügige Räume, mit ca. 152 m² Wfl. und ca.
666 m² Grdst., gepflegter Zustand. Inkl. Ga-
rage und PKW-Stellpl. Bezug sofort möglich.
Wolfgang Wagner 07142 594-352

B

Bauen mit Freude
www.massivhaus-boxler.de
Massivhaus Boxler GmbH
Bahnhofstraße 49 + 60
87724 Ottobeuren
Tel. 08332/93001
Fax 08332/93060
info@massivhaus-boxler.de

DAS MASSIVHAUS
IN ZIEGEL- ODER HOLZBAUWEISE

● auf Ihrem Grundstück
● individuelle Planung
● Ausbauhaus
● schlüsselfertig
● zum Festpreis

Hausbesichtigung im Internet!
Fordern Sie unseren Farbprospekt an!

C

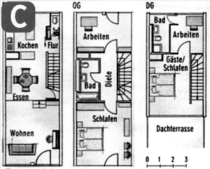

Grundrisse 121 qm auf 3 Etagen,
plus 68 qm im Keller. Zwei Roll-
container ergänzen die Küchenzeile.

D

Für die ganze Familie!
Bönnigheim € 265.000,–
Gepflegte Doppelhaushälfte, in ruhiger
Ortsrandlage, mit ca. 125 m² Wfl. und ca.
520 m² Grdst., Bj. 1968. Die Ausstattung
entspricht teilweise dem Baujahr. Mit
Wintergarten, Süd-/Westausrichtung. Inkl.
Doppelgarage und Einzelgarage. Frei ab
August
Tina Teschke 07142 594-351

E

F

...tzimmer
...eleichten Oberflächen in
...tur, Kunststoff-Nachbildung.
Drehtürenschrank, 2-türig, 1 Spiegel,
Maß ca. 150x201x64 cm,
Einzelbett, LF ca. 100x200 cm,
Nachtkonsole, mit 3 Schubkästen.
Art. Nr. 112744

*Alle Preise ohne
Lattenroste,
Matratzen, Auflagen
und Dekoration*

Liegehöhe gleich
Sitzhöhe!

G

Liegewiese
Aus eins mach drei: Wie ein
Bausatz lässt sich das
Sofa durch Umstecken
und Umklappen in ein
Einzel- oder Doppelbett
verwandeln. „MR 810",
176 x 96 cm; Liegefläche
150 cm. 958€. Musterring.

H

Bietigheim
Otto-Hahn-Straße Ⓢ
Im Innenausbau

Traumhaft
idyllisch wohnen
im Ellental

Ihr Projektleiter
Herr Axel Bellon
0151 / 15913771

Hier läßt es sich leben!
3½- Zimmer-
Wohnung mit
riesigem Balkon
€ 162.800,–

So finden Sie unsere Baustellen: Von Stadtmitte erst Ri. Sachsen-
heim, an Kreuzung geradeaus, Ri. Eissporthalle, 2. Möglichkeit re. rein.

Beispiele aus unserem Angebot:
2½ Zimmer, Balkon € 104.800,-
3½ Zimmer, Garten € 145.800,-
4½ Zimmer, Mais. € 169.800,-
4½ Zimmer, Garten € 209.800,-

I

Viel Platz – nicht nur für Hund und Katz!
Kornwestheim € 369.000,–
3-Familienhaus, ca. 216 m² Wfl. und ca. 560 m²
Grdst., Bj. 1970. 4 Balkone, großer Garten und
Doppelgarage. Dach 2005 gedeckt und iso-
liert. Ansonsten weitestgehend baujahrsty-
pischer Zustand. Frei nach Vereinbarung.
Markus Barho 07145 209-29

J

Verwirklichen Sie Ihren Traum!
Remseck-Aldingen € 379.000,–
2-Familienhaus mit ca. 188 m² Wfl. und ca.
812 m² Grdst., Bj. 1961, in gewachsenem
Wohngebiet. Ausstattung entspricht dem
Baujahr. Beziehbar nach Vereinbarung.
Markus Barho 07145 209-29

K **Look at the ads of the houses and apartments for sale, rent or building. Match the letter of each picture with the appropriate description. This property. . .**

___ 1. is 121 square meters big and has three floors.

___ 2. shows custom-made houses built by the *Massivhaus* Company.

___ 3. is located in the *Otto-Hahn-Straße*.

___ 4. is the most expensive one listed.

___ 5. is a 2-family house built in 1961.

___ 6. is one-half of a double house and is available in August.

___ 7. is a 3-family house with four balconies.

L **Give the German name of each room associated with**

1. picture E: _____

2. picture F: _____

3. picture G: _____

Symtalk

M **Ergänze die richtigen Wörter auf Deutsch!** *(In the space, write the correct word in German.)*

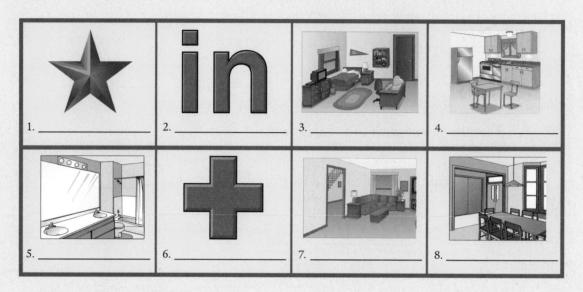

1. _____
2. _____
3. _____
4. _____
5. _____
6. _____
7. _____
8. _____

N **Sag die Sätze! Dann schreib sie auf Deutsch!** *(Say the sentences, then write them in German.)*

1. _____

2. _____

3. _____

4. _____

Mit einem Klassenkameraden, stell die Frage oder gib die Antwort! *(With a classmate, ask the question or give the answer. Then, write the dialogue.)*

1.

_____

2.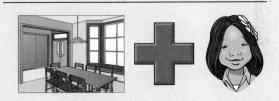

_____

3.

_____

4.

_____

5.

_____

Kreuzworträtsel

Waagerecht

2. where
5. place to prepare meals
7. _____ *haus,* a house for one family
9. *Wo _____ du?*
11. small house in the country or woods
12. canvas camping shelter
13. paved outdoor area for relaxing

Senkrecht

1. place to play or grow flowers
2. rental unit
3. large luxurious house
4. place to bathe
6. *Wie viele Zimmer _____ es in deinem Haus?*
8. found in all houses or apartments
10. behind
11. place to reside

UNIT 6

Die Familie

Family

Vokabeln

die Großeltern
grandparents

die Großmutter
grandmother

der Großvater
grandfather

der Mann
husband

die Eltern
parents

die Frau
wife

der Onkel
uncle

die Tante
aunt

der Vater
father

die Mutter
mother

die Kinder
children

die Schwester
sister

der Bruder
brother

die Nichte
niece

die Kusine
cousin

der Neffe
nephew

der Cousin
cousin

der Sohn
son

der Enkel
grandson

die Tochter
daughter

die Enkelin
granddaughter

Wer ist das?
Who is this?

Das ist mein Bruder.
It's my brother.

Sind das deine Eltern?
Are they your parents?

Ja, meine Mutter heißt Jutta und mein Vater heißt Josef.
Yes. My mother's name is Jutta and my father's name is Josef.

Wer sind die Kinder?
Who are the children?

Sie sind mein Enkel und meine Enkelin.
They're my granddaughter and my grandson.

Leonie, Sabine, und Alexander sind Schwestern und Bruder, nicht wahr?
Leonie, Sabine, and Andreas are sisters and brother, aren't they?

Ja, und sie sind auch meine Kusinen.
Yes, and they are also my cousins.

**Vergiss nicht!
Familientreffen
Gäste**

Don't forget!
Family Reunion
Guests

- **Tante Anneliese und ihr Mann**
  Aunt Anneliese and her husband

- **meine Schwester und ihre Kinder**
  my sister and her children

- **Onkel Willi und seine Frau**
  Uncle Willi and his wife

- **Diana und das Baby**
  Diana and the baby

Niklas: **Wo sind deine Verwandten?**
Where are your relatives?

Simon: **Meine Großeltern sind drinnen und meine Tanten und Onkel sind im Garten.**
My grandparents are inside, and my uncles and aunts are in the garden.

❀❀❀❀❀

Laura: **Sind deine Paten hier?**
Are your godparents here?

Dieter: **Ja, sicher. Meine Patin spricht gerade mit meinen Tanten. Mein Pate ist auf der Terrasse.**
Yes, of course! My godmother is speaking with my aunts. My godfather is on the terrace.

Extra Vokabeln

das Kind
child (male)

der Junge
boy

das Kind
child (female)

der Mann
man (as well as husband)

das Mädchen
girl

die Frau
woman
(as well as wife)

das Baby
baby
(male or female)

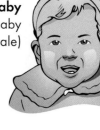

der Stiefbruder stepbrother	**der Stiefvater** stepfather	**der Stiefsohn** stepson
die Stiefschwester stepsister	**die Stiefmutter** stepmother	**die Stieftochter** stepdaughter

 Godparents play an important part in a child's life. Their main role is to offer encouragement and spiritual guidance as the child grows. On special occasions they often remember their godchild with a small gift.

Übungen

A Indicate Leonie's relationship to each family member listed.

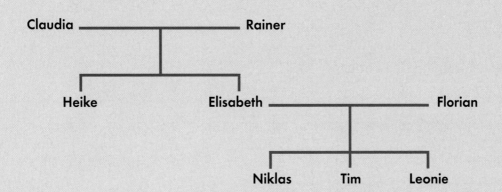

Leonie ist die. . .

1. _____ von Tim.
2. _____ von Elisabeth.
3. _____ von Rainer.
4. _____ von Niklas.
5. _____ von Claudia.
6. _____ von Heike.
7. _____ von Florian.

B Tu das Gleiche für Elisabeth und Rainer! *(Do the same for Elisabeth and Rainer.)*

Elisabeth ist die. . .

1. _____ von Niklas, Tim und Leonie.
2. _____ von Florian.
3. _____ von Heike.
4. _____ von Claudia und Rainer.

Rainer ist der. . .

5. _____ von Claudia.
6. _____ von Heike und Elisabeth.
7. _____ von Niklas, Tim und Leonie.

Wer ist das? *(Who is that?)* **Schreib auf Deutsch, bitte!**

> **Beispiel:** Der Bruder von meinem Vater
> ist mein Onkel.

1. Die Schwester von meinem Vater

   _____

2. Der Sohn von meinem Bruder

   _____

3. Der Vater von meinem Vater

   _____

4. Die Mutter von meiner Mutter

   _____

5. Die Tochter von meiner Tante

   _____

D **Wer bin ich?** *(Who am I?)* **Schreib auf Deutsch, bitte!**

1. I am your father's son. I am your

   _____

2. I am your cousin's mother. I am your

   _____

3. I am your father's brother. I am your

   _____

4. I am your mother's father. I am your

   _____

E **Wähle die richtige Antwort!** *(Choose the correct answer.)*

1. Wo sind die Großeltern?
   A. in the crib
   B. next to the crib
   C. in the foreground

2. Wo sind die Eltern?
   A. next to the crib
   B. in the crib
   C. in the foreground

3. Wo ist das Kind?
   A. next to the crib
   B. in the crib
   C. in the foreground

F **Schreib auf Englisch!** *(What do these questions mean in English?)*

1. Wer ist das?

_____

2. Wer bin ich?

_____

3. Wer ist der Mann?

_____

4. Wer spricht mit Tante Anneliese?

_____

G **Complete in German the answers to the following questions. Use the cues in parentheses.**

1. Wer ist der Junge? *(son)* Er ist mein _____.

2. Wer ist die Frau? *(aunt)* Sie ist meine _____.

3. Wer ist das Baby? *(brother)* Es ist mein _____.

H **Read the passage, and then translate it into English. Just guess at the words you may not know! See how much you can figure out!**

> *Ich habe* eine *kleine* Familie. Mein Vater ist siebenunddreißig Jahre alt. Meine Mutter ist achtunddreißig Jahre alt. Meine Schwester heißt Tanja und sie ist neun. Mein Bruder heißt Dieter und er ist sechs. Ich heiße Alex und ich bin dreizehn. Meine Familie wohnt in Berlin. *Wir haben* ein Haus. Meine Großeltern wohnen in Leipzig. *Sie haben* eine Wohnung.

Ich habe I have   **Wir/Sie haben** we/they have
kleine small

_____

_____

_____

_____

_____

_____

_____

I Zum Sprechen. **Ask your speaking partner about five members of his/her family. Ask about the name and age of each person. Your partner should answer each question. Then he/she will ask you about your family, and you will answer.**

> Beispiel: A: Hast du einen Bruder? *(Do you have a brother?)*
> B: Ja, ich habe einen Bruder.
> A: Wie heißt er? *(What is his name?)*
> B: Er heißt Daniel.
> A: Wie alt ist er? *(How old is he?)*
> B: Er ist fünfzehn.

J Du bist dran! **Find some family photographs and exchange them with a friend. Holding up your friend's photo first, ask him/her who is in the picture. He/she will identify each person with the correct relationship. Then, reverse roles.**

> Beispiel: A: Wer ist das? *(Who is this?)*
> B: Das ist meine Großmutter. *(That's my grandmother.)*

A

Unseren lieben Eltern

Lieselotte und Erich Bankmann

zur Goldenen Hochzeit

die herzlichsten Wünsche
bei guter Gesundheit von euren
sieben Kindern

*Monika, Bärbel, Karin,
Angelika, Beate, Petra, Tonio
sowie allen Enkelkindern, Urenkeln
und Lebenspartnern*

Warnemünde, 20. April

B

Lieber Ammergau-Opa!
Herzlichen Glückwunsch zu
deinem morgigen
70. Geburtstag
von deiner Frau Elfriede

deinen Töchtern
Conny
mit **Nino**
und **Alexandra**

und

Claudia
mit **Pit**
Thomas und **Stefan**

C

Mit 70
so attraktiv wie
mit 17
Zu Deinem 70. Geburtstag,
liebe Christel,
wünschen wir alles Gute,
Gesundheit und Wohlergehen auf immer und ewig,
Herbert Bartle, Jürgen und Monika, Rainer und Birgit, Mara Lena,
Philipp und Felix, Martina, Manfred und Christa, Klaus und Ute,
Margarete, Inge, Elfriede und der Rote Schorsch.

D

Liebe Ingrid,

Alles erdenklich Liebe und Gute zu
Deinem Geburtstag.
Wir sind glücklich und stolz, dass wir Dich
haben.
Bleib weiter, wie Du bist.
Deine Eltern

40 ♡ 40 ♡ 40 ♡ 40 ♡ 40 ♡ 40 ♡ 40 ♡ 40 ♡ 40 ♡ 40 ♡ 40

E

Liebe Imke!
Alles Gute zum
18. Geburtstag.
Bin froh, dass es Dich gibt.
Annika

F

Lieber Papa
Werner Müller

Alles, alles gute zum
80. Geburtstag,
viel Glück und Gesundheit
wünschen Dir

Deine Schwiegertochter
Maya, Dein Sohn Reinhard,
Deine Enkelin Katharina

G

Wir
heiraten
heute

Jasmin Friedrich
Michael Messe

Bad Harzburg
Breite Straße 133
Schlewecker Trift 2 a

H

Liebe Oma Helga
und Opa Günter,
herzlich willkommen
daheim!

K *Wer ist das?* Look at the congratulatory ads and then match the letter for each ad to the person described. Some letters may be used more than once. This person/these persons. . .

___ 1. is 40 years old.

___ 2. has a daughter named Claudia.

___ 3. and her spouse are welcomed home by their grandchildren.

___ 4. are congratulated by their seven children on their golden wedding anniversary.

___ 5. has a wife named Elfriede.

___ 6. celebrates a birthday as a teenager.

___ 7. has a son named Reinhard.

___ 8. are celebrating a special occasion in the spring.

___ 9. is shown in a current photo and in a photo from 53 years ago.

___ 10. are getting married today.

___ 11. is congratulated by her parents.

___ 12. has one granddaughter.

L Ask three of your classmates these questions: *Hast du einen Bruder? Wie heißt er? Hast du eine Schwester? Wie heißt sie?* After you have jotted down their answers, write out your final findings in sentence form. If your classmate does not have a brother or sister, use the form of *kein*. Follow this example:

> **Beispiel:** *(name of classmate)* hat einen/keinen Bruder.
> *(name of classmate)* hat eine/keine Schwester.

Sprichwort

Der Apfel fällt nicht weit vom Stamm.
A chip off the old block.

Symtalk

M **Ergänze die richtigen Wörter auf Deutsch!** *(In the space, write the correct word in German.)*

1. _____   2. _____   3. _____   4. _____   5. _____   6. _____

N **Sag die Sätze! Dann schreib sie auf Deutsch!** *(Say the sentences, then write them in German.)*

1. _____

2. _____

3. _____

4. _____

O **Mit einem Klassenkameraden, stell die Frage oder gib die Antwort!** *(With a classmate, ask the question or give the answer. Then, write the dialogue.)*

1.

_____   _____

2.

_____   _____

3.

_____   _____

4.

_____   _____

5.

_____   _____

Kreuzworträtsel

Waagerecht

1. Meine ____ ist die Tochter von meiner Tante und meinem Onkel.
3. Herr Weber ist ein ____.
5. Mein ____ ist der Mann von meiner Mutter.
8. Frau Schubert ist eine ____.
9. Mein ____ ist der Bruder von meinem Vater.
10. Mein ____ ist der Sohn von meinem Vater und meiner Mutter.
11. Eine Mutter, ein Vater und Kinder sind eine ____.

Senkrecht

2. Eberhard ist der ____ von seinen (his) Eltern.
4. Mein ____ ist der Sohn von meiner Schwester.
5. Meine Onkel, Tanten, Cousins und Großeltern sind meine ____.
6. Maja ist die ____ von ihren (her) Eltern.
7. Meine ____ ist die Frau von meinem Vater.

UNIT 7

Die Tiere

Animals

Vokabeln

die Kuh
cow

der Esel
donkey

der Vogel
bird

die Ente
duck

das Schwein
pig

der Hahn
rooster

die Henne
hen

die Katze
cat (female)

das Pferd
horse

der Hund
dog (male)

JUTTA:	Komm mit, Simon! Ich füttre jetzt die Tiere. Ich gebe Max einen Apfel. *Come on, Simon! I'm feeding the animals now. I'm giving Max an apple.*
SIMON:	Schön! Ich möchte helfen. *Great! I'd like to help you.*
JUTTA:	Ja, sicher, Simon. Du kannst den Eimer halten. *Of course you can, Simon! You can hold the pail.*
SIMON:	Wie heißt die Katze? *What's the cat's name?*
JUTTA:	Das ist Miezi. *That's Miezi.*
SIMON:	Gibt es auch Hennen? *Are there hens, too?*
JUTTA:	Ja, viele! Sie sind hinter der Scheune. Du kannst die Eier sammeln. *Yes, they're behind the barn. You can collect the eggs.*

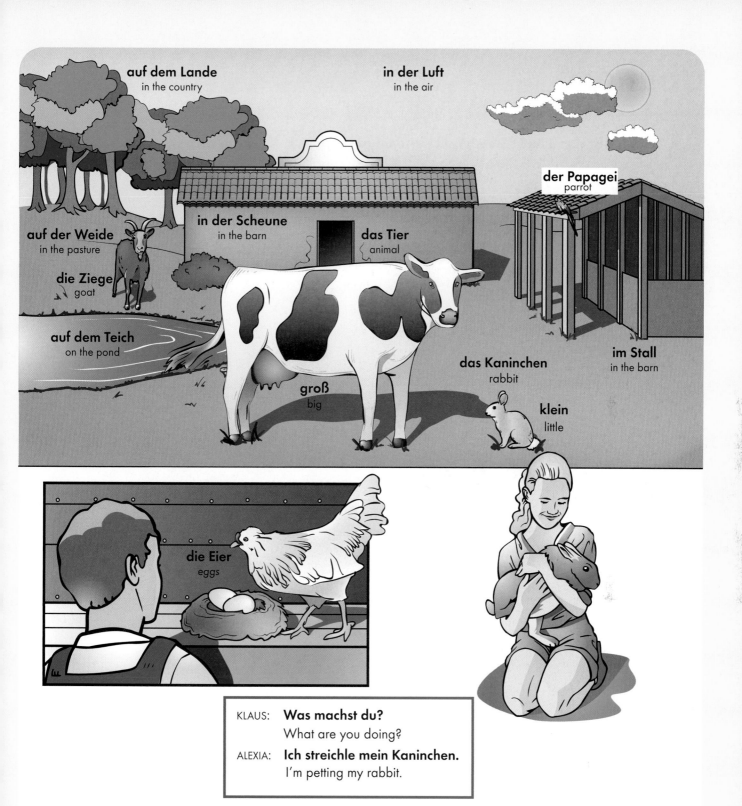

auf dem Lande
in the country

in der Luft
in the air

der Papagei
parrot

in der Scheune
in the barn

das Tier
animal

auf der Weide
in the pasture

die Ziege
goat

auf dem Teich
on the pond

groß
big

das Kaninchen
rabbit

im Stall
in the barn

klein
little

die Eier
eggs

KLAUS:	**Was machst du?**
	What are you doing?
ALEXIA:	**Ich streichle mein Kaninchen.**
	I'm petting my rabbit.

Sounds that animals make:

Die Kuh sagt **muh** (moo).

Das Pferd sagt **hü ü ü ü** (neigh).

Die Katze sagt **miau** (meow).

Der Hund sagt **wau wau / wuff wuff** (woof).

Das Schwein sagt **grunz** (oink).

Die Ente sagt **quack quack** (quack).

Der Hahn sagt **kickeriki** (cock-a-doodle-doo).

Übungen

A **Wie heißt das Tier?** *(Identify each animal in German.)*

1. Das ist eine _____.

2. Das ist eine _____.

3. Das ist ein _____.

4. Das ist ein _____.

5. Das ist ein _____.

Welches Tier ist. . .? *(Which animal can usually be found at each location?)* **Schreib auf Deutsch bitte!**

1. auf der Weide:

   _____

2. im Stall:

   _____

3. auf dem Teich:

   _____

4. in der Luft:

   _____

5. in der Scheune:

   _____

C **Wo? Wer? Was? Wähle die richtige Antwort!** *(Where? Who? What? Which? Choose the correct answer.)*

1. Wo sind Jutta und Simon?
   A. auf dem Teich
   B. auf der Weide
   C. auf dem Lande

2. Wo ist das Pferd?
   A. in der Luft
   B. im Stall
   C. auf dem Teich

3. Wer hat einen Apfel für Max?
   A. Jutta
   B. Simon
   C. das Pferd

4. Wer möchte helfen?
   A. Jutta
   B. Simon
   C. Miezi

5. Was hat Jutta?
   A. eine Kuh
   B. eine Ziege
   C. einen Eimer

6. Was ist klein?
   A. ein Vogel
   B. ein Esel
   C. eine Kuh

D **Ergänze die Sätze richtig.** *(Complete the sentences correctly.)*

___ 1. Die Katze heißt _____.

___ 2. Der Esel ist _____.

___ 3. Die Kuh ist auf der _____.

___ 4. Der Apfel ist für _____.

___ 5. Die Ente ist _____.

A. Max

B. klein

C. groß

D. Miezi

E. Weide

E **Rearrange this group of animals. Start with the smallest in size and end with the biggest.**

Kuh　　　　Kaninchen　　　　Ziege　　　　Vogel

1. _____　　3. _____

2. _____　　4. _____

F **What is each animal like? Indicate the size of each animal by choosing either little *(klein)* or big *(groß)*. Write out the full sentence in German.**

Beispiel:　A: Wie ist ein Pferd?
　　　　　　　Ein Pferd ist groß.

1. Wie ist ein Esel?

_____

2. Wie ist eine Katze?

_____

3. Wie ist eine Ziege?

_____

4. Wie ist ein Schwein?

_____

5. Wie ist ein Vogel?

_____

G **What goes together? Match the German with the English. Focus on the familiar words and guess the others.**

____ 1. Ich bin auf dem Lande.

____ 2. Ich sehe die Tiere.

____ 3. Ich möchte helfen.

____ 4. Ich kann den Eimer halten.

____ 5. Ich füttre die Katze.

____ 6. Ich kann die Eier sammeln.

A. I see the animals.

B. I would like to help.

C. I can collect the eggs.

D. I'm feeding the cat.

E. I can hold the pail.

F. I am in the country.

H **Zum Sprechen. Select four animals from this unit. Ask your speaking partner where each one is. He/she should answer correctly. Then, your partner asks you where four other animals are. You reply this time.**

> Beispiel: A: Wo ist die Ente?
> B: Die Ente ist auf dem Teich.

I **Du bist dran! Find out whether your classmate knows the names of the animals. Offer a clue for each animal, such as sounds or actions: It oinks; it neighs; it meows; it barks; it moos; it warbles; it climbs; it swims; it gives eggs; it carries loads, or it twitches its whiskers. Make sure your classmate says _der_ or _die_ or _das_ before each name. Next, your partner will give you a clue by saying a location, such as pasture, pond, stall, air, or barn. You will say in German the name of the animal associated with each place.**

Lebendige Sprache

A — Tiermarkt

Frische Hühner- und Enteneier zu verkaufen 015114158721

Kaninchen zu verkaufen 015114158721

Verschiedene Hühner (Sumatra,Brahmer,Vorwerk,Rhodeländer,Lakenfelder,Cochin usw.) weiße Zwergenten, Wildenten, Nonnengänse, Nilgänse, Pfauenhennen zu verkaufen 015114158721

8 Monate altes Rosettenmeerschweinchen mit gut erh. Innenstall und Zubehör für 20 € in gute Hände abzugeben ☎ 0 25 72/20 94 77

2 Chinchilla Weibchen (ca. 2 u. 3 J.) mit großem Holzkäfig (ca. BTH 100x80x150 cm) und viel Zubehör nur in gute Hände abzugeben; VB 120 € ☎ 0176/24257065

Schicker 6-jähriger Rappwallach von Dynast, 167 cm Stm., gute GGA, super Springvermögen, VB 5000 € ☎ 0170-3536360

15 kleine Kaninchen á 5 € u. 3 gr. Kaninchen á 10 € zu verkaufen. ☎ 02572/8 87 02

B — Pferde / Reitsport

Pferdebox frei, mit Weidegang und Verpflegung, ohne Kraftfutter, 100 € in Emsdetten. ☎ 02572/49 34

11-jähr. holst. Wallach, leichtr., schwarzbraun, absolut brav & ehrl. am Sprung & im Umgang, A gew., L platz, auch für Umsteiger geeignet, VB, ☎ 0176-20 52 11 61

Ponykutsche auf Shetty eingestellt, leichtlaufend, 2-achsig, 4-sitzig, 350 € FP, ☎ 02575/9 71 98 88 (Praxis)

Isländer zu verkaufen, 8-jähr. Wallach, Vater: Tritell von Berlar, dunkelbraun, sehr lieb. ☎ 01 77/1 44 31 93

Cavallo Lederreitstiefel Gr. 8 (42); Höhe 52, Weite 38 m.Reißverschluß; links a.d. Ferse einmal prof. geflickt; fällt kaum auf; gut erhalten!!! VB 90 € MS 9873534

2er Pferdeanhänger, defekt für 600,-€ zu verkaufen. ☎ 01 71/3 25 12 38

C — Vögel und Fische

Skalare, versch. Farben aus Hobbyzucht abzugeben, Stck. 2,50 € ☎ 02 51/62 41 83 AB

Chin. Zwergwachteln (nur Hähne) zu verschenken. ☎ ab Mittwoch. 02582/8564.

1 Streifenwels und 1 Netz-Schmerle, 10 Stck. Feenbarsche, zu verk., VB, ☎ 02504/7157

2 x Gloster Hähne, je 12 €, 2 x Kanarienhähne je 9 € zu verkaufen. ☎ 0 25 72/10 20

20 Stck. Zebrafinken für 20 € abzugeben. ☎ 0 25 72/8 05 36

Zwergschachbrett-Schmerle sucht ihres Gleichen, entweder zu Artgenossen zu verschenken oder weitere Tiere zu kaufen gesucht. ☎ 0251/1364063

6 Zwergpanzerwelse zu verschenken, artgerechte Haltung wird vorausgesetzt. Tiere werden gebracht. Zwergsachbrett-Schmerle sucht ihres Gleichen. ☎ 0251/1364063

Ausstellungskäfige für Wellensittiche + Transportkartons 5 Stck. für 50 € zu verk. ☎ 02571/5760732.

Birmingham Roller und Wiener Hochflieger, Jungtiere abzugeben, Emsdetten, ☎ 0 25 72/ 68 04

Ca. 50 Goldfische (versch. Größen) preisgünstig zu verk., ☎ 02582/8427

Diamanttäubchen für nur St. 10 € oder Paar für 18 € ☎ 0 25 72/50 39

Flugenten abzugeben. 0 59 73/21 41

D — Hunde und Katzen

Airedale-Terrier-Welpen suchen ab Mitte Juni ein liebevolles Zuhause! (Hobbyzucht m. P., KfT, VDH) 0160/90152971 Münster/Greven

Labrador-Welpen, schwarz, o.P., toller Wurf, klasse Eltern, Vater m.P., geimpft u. entwurmt, ab 10.05.06 zu verkaufen. ☎ 02507-91 74, 0175-2 16 39 96 ab 16 Uhr

Beaglewelpen ab 25.Mai abzugeben, tricolor, entwurmt, in Fam. aufgewachsen. 350.-€ /Welpe. ☎ 02564/66 03

Suche gut erh. Fahrrad Hundeanhänger mit Anhängerkupplung für jedes Fahrrad. Angebote an ☎ 0 25 73/95 56 78

Hundekorb Ca.110X80cm kaum gebraucht 30€ Tel 02501/8647

Bildschöne Rauhaarteckel, DTK-Papiere, zu verkaufen. ☎ 05459/93200 www.teckel-sunderhaar.de

Button, eine total verspielte u. verschmuste braungetigerte Katze v. 9 Mon., sucht ein Zuhause mit Auslauf. Sie mag andere Katzen, Hunde u. versteht sich sehr gut m. Kindern. Katzenhilfe Münster ☎ 0251/8 46 97 57

Hovawart-Welpen, sehr menschenbezogen und gut sozialisiert in liebevolle Hände abzugeben. ☎ 02534/1691

Oskar, ein liebenswerter getigerter Kater v. 1,5 Jahren, geimpft, kastriert u. Wohnungshaltung gewöhnt, sucht mit seiner bildhübschen Freundin (Mischling) „Momo" ein gemeinsames Zuhause. ☎ 0251/8 46 97 57

Schäferhund-Mischling in gute Hände zu verk. ☎ 01 76/51 23 34 77

Schöne Jack-Russel-Welpen, entwurmt u. geimpft, suchen ein neues Zuhause. ☎ 0 25 72/35 74

Sisal-Kratztonne, Höhe ca. 85 cm, ø 30 cm, mehrere Eingänge u. Liegefläche, standfest durch große Bodenplatte, absolut neu, 48,- €; 2 sehr große Kratzbretter, Sisal, neu. ☎ 0170/5553438

Suche kostenlos od. günstig einen Hund, Miniaturbullterrier. In gute Hände. ☎ 0251/1 44 37 17

Verkaufe komplettes Katzenzubehör für 25,- €. ☎ 02534/64 54 69

J As is customary in their country, Germans advertise when they want to buy or sell animals or related items. Write the letter A, B, C, or D when you have identified the section to which the described sentence refers.

_____ 1. Chickens and other animals are being sold. If you want to buy any of the listed animals, you can call this phone number: 015114158721.

_____ 2. Beagles are being sold after May 25.

_____ 3. About 50 goldfish in different sizes are being offered for sale.

_____ 4. A pony carriage is for sale for 350 euros.

_____ 5. Ducks are offered by calling 0 59 73/21 41.

_____ 6. This person is selling fresh chicken and duck eggs.

_____ 7. A dog basket will be sold for 30 euros.

_____ 8. Two canaries can be bought for nine euros each.

_____ 9. An eleven-year-old black and brown gelding *(Wallach)* is for sale.

_____ 10. Oskar is a tomcat.

_____ 11. More than a dozen rabbits are for sale.

_____ 12. A person is looking for a miniature bullterrier free of charge.

K Rearrange the letters below to find six animals.

1. Z K E T A: _____

2. C W N S I H E: _____

3. R F D P E: _____

4. T E E N: _____

5. G O V E L: _____

6. H K U: _____

Sprichwort

Wenn die Katze aus dem Haus ist, tanzen die Mäuse.
When the cat's away, the mice will play.

Symtalk

L Ergänze die richtigen Wörter auf Deutsch! *(In the space, write the correct word in German.)*

1. _____

2. _____

3. _____

4. _____

5. _____

6. _____

M Frage und beantworte die Fragen auf Deutsch! *(Ask and answer the questions in German.)*

1.

_____ _____

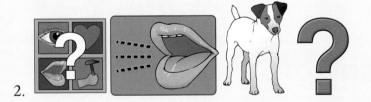

2.

_____ _____

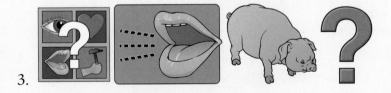

3.

_____ _____

N **Work with a partner. After one of you asks the question, the other responds that no, the person likes a different kind of animal. Please write the dialogue in German.**

1.

_____

Nein, _____

2.

_____

Nein, _____

3.

_____

Nein, _____

4.

_____

Nein, _____

5.

_____

Nein, _____

Kreuzworträtsel

Waagerecht

2. source of our milk
3. purrs and has soft fur
5. water bird
7. a popular house pet
8. farm building
10. animals' resting place
12. what equestrians ride

Senkrecht

1. flies in the air
2. loves to eat vegetable gardens
4. small body of water
6. stubborn animal
9. container
11. where the *Vogel* likes to be

UNIT 8

Die Berufe

Occupations

Vokabeln

**der Künstler
die Künstlerin**
artist

**der Geschäftsmann
die Geschäftsfrau**
businessman, businesswoman

**der Elektriker
die Elektrikerin**
electrician

**der Tischler
die Tischlerin**
carpenter

**der Koch
die Köchin**
cook

**der Krankenpfleger
die Krankenpflegerin**
nurse

**der Mechaniker
die Mechanikerin**
mechanic

**der Arzt
die Ärztin**
physician

**der Musiker
die Musikerin**
musician

**der Lehrer
die Lehrerin**
teacher

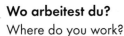

**der Landwirt
die Landwirtin**
farmer

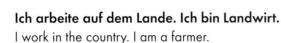

**der Briefträger
die Briefträgerin**
letter carrier

**der Klempner
die Klempnerin**
plumber

**der Programmierer
die Programmiererin**
computer programmer

Wo arbeitest du?
Where do you work?

Ich arbeite auf dem Lande. Ich bin Landwirt.
I work in the country. I am a farmer.

- The German school system provides an excellent vocational education program. Students combine class work with actual on-the-job training. A vocational school is called a *Berufsschule*.
- *die Arbeit*: work; *die Arbeitsstelle*: job, position of employment

Arbeitest du gern?
Do you like to work?

Ja. Ich arbeite gern.
Yes, I like to work.

Was machst du?
What do you do (for a living)?

Ich bin Schauspielerin. Ich arbeite im Theater.
I am an actress. I work at the theater.

Was ist dein Beruf?
What is your occupation?

Ich bin Schauspieler.
I am an actor.

Übungen

A Number in order the professions or trades as your teacher says each one.

_____ die Ärztin   _____ der Lehrer

_____ der Geschäftsmann   _____ die Mechanikerin

_____ die Künstlerin   _____ der Koch

_____ der Landwirt   _____ der Programmierer

_____ die Briefträgerin   _____ die Musikerin

B Wer arbeitet hier? *(Who works here?)*

1. stage _____

2. dairy barn _____

3. post office _____

4. orchestra pit _____

5. sales office _____

6. hospital _____

7. restaurant _____

8. wood shop _____

9. school _____

10. auto service station _____

C Schreib die Wörter richtig! *(Unscramble the letters to show five occupations.)*

1. RELRHE _____

2. TIRDWALN _____

3. ITZÄRN _____

4. INCHÖK _____

5. PAEERRRRMMIOG _____

D **Ergänze die Sätze!** *(Complete the sentences by using the cues in parentheses.)*

1. Was ist dein _____? *(occupation)*

2. Ich _____ Koch. *(am)*

3. Ich_____ in der Küche. *(work)*

4. Wo arbeitest _____, Abdul? *(you)*

5. _____ arbeite bei der Post. *(I)*

6. Was _____ du? *(What do you do?)*

7. Ich bin _____. *(letter carrier)*

8. Ich arbeite _____. *(I like to work.)*

E **Wie heißt das auf Englisch?** *(How do you say this in English? Look first, then take a good guess. Write out each sentence in English.)*

1. Meine Mutter ist Lehrerin.

   _____

2. Sie lehrt in einer Schule.

   _____

3. Mein Vater ist Musiker.

   _____

4. Er spielt Flöte.

   _____

5. Meine Kusine ist Programmiererin.

   _____

6. Sie arbeitet mit einem Computer.

   _____

7. Mein Cousin ist Koch.

   _____

8. Er arbeitet in einem Restaurant.

   _____

F **Wer ist das?** *(Guess who. . .?)* **Auf Deutsch, bitte.**

1. Der _____ creates software.

2. Die _____ is in charge of the (medical) operation.

3. Der _____ checks for faulty wiring.

4. Die _____ installs wooden beams.

5. Der _____ paints portraits.

6. Die _____ cooks food.

7. Der _____ manages a company.

8. Die _____ milks cows.

9. Der _____ delivers mail.

10. Die _____ plays in a symphony orchestra.

G **Schreib einen Beruf zu jeder Abbildung!** *(Write the name of an occupation for each illustration.)*

1. _____

2. _____

3. _____

4. _____

5. _____

H   **Zum Sprechen!** Take turns with your speaking partner. Give each other five cues each as to a person's occupation. For example: You say "hospital" and your partner will say: *der Arzt/die Ärztin.* Then she gives you a cue, such as "paintbrush" and you will say: *der Künstler/die Künstlerin.*

I   **Du bist dran!** Help create a classroom bulletin board display about occupations. Cut out pictures from magazines showing people in all the occupations listed in this Unit. Label each one in German, for example: *Das ist ein Koch*, or *Das ist eine Briefträgerin.* Label the entire display as *Berufe.*

Koch/Pizzabäcker/in
für Gaststätte
in Besigheim gesucht.
Große Wohnung ist vorhanden.
Kontakt: Tel. 01 62-9 64 65 27

Koch
Berufseinsteiger sucht Festanstellung
(TZ möglich), im Raum Berlin.
Telefon: 0171 - 206 73 77

Suche Jungkoch
für Gasthaus in Nußdorf/Austria
ab Oktober ganztägig.
Telefon 0043/664/4533422

!!! **Suchen ab** Juli erfahrene, zuverlässige Telefonistin, 400,- € Basis, Arbeitzeit: Nachts!!! ✉ BR Z 117564

Arbeiten von zu Hause - freie Zeiteinteilung, haupt- oder nebenberuflich. www.pcarbeit-nebenjob.de

Dr. B. M.-Obradovic
Fachärztin für Allgemeinmedizin
Akupunktur, Homöopathie
Ernährungsmedizin, Mesotherapie
Stuttgarter Str. 32, 71638 Ludwigsburg

Arzthelferin
für Teilzeit ab sofort gesucht
Telefon (0 71 41) 9 13 11 24

Su. Verkäufer/innen für Imbiß in Teilzeit. Näheres unter ✆ 0179/6737803

Selbst. Maler (28) su. Anstellung i. Mü.-STA Ammersee, evtl. auch SUB-Untern., Stunden-Basis, Hausbetreuung-Pflege od. Chauffeur, zuverl.u. flex. ☎ 0179/1262769

ArchitekturDesign-Studentin sucht Nebentätigkeit im Bereich Theater, Kultur, Kunst, Design(...) in München ☎089/45247275 Kontakt gern per Mail leoniedroste@web.de

Arzthelferin, mögl. mit Röntgenkenntnissen, für orthopädische Praxis in Dresden gesucht. Bewerbungen bitte unter ✉ 36133 A 'SZ' 01045 DD

Maler su. Tapezier-/Malerarbeiten
0171/2621423 o. 09543/443595

Bürogehilfin
Sucht Teilzeitarbeit,
MS-Office-Kenntnisse.
#22-9970, Morgenpost, 10445 Berlin

Flexibler Automobilverkäufer aus ungekündigter Stellung sucht neuen Wirkungskreis. Angebote bitte unter: ✉ 36216 Z 'SZ' 01045 DD

Bäcker/in für Mini-Job (2 Tage) in Holzofenbackstube in 01848 Hohnstein gesucht ☎ /Fax: 035975/80302

Sie, 52 J., Köchin, s. Job in Bistro, Imbiss o. Kiosk, auch Prod. oder berufsfr. Tätigk., Schicht mögl., ab ca. 35 h/Woche. ☎ 0351-4224624

Sekretärin, m. s. guten Buchh.-Kenntn., su. Aufgabe im Finanzbereich, langj. Erf., Zuverlässigk., Kompetenz u.Verhandlungsgeschick (a. Teilzt./std.weise) **08142/506044**

J **Review these employment ads and answer the following questions.**

1. How many ads are there for cooks?

   _____

2. What is the name of the city where Dr. B.M.-Obradovic's dentistry is located?

   _____

3. For how many days per week does the bakery need a baker?

   _____

4. What is the phone number for the restaurant in Besigheim that is looking for a cook?

   _____

5. How old is the painter *(Maler)* who is looking for a job?

   _____

6. Where does the person looking for a part-time office assistant's *(Bürogehilfin)* job live?

   _____

7. For what job is the person whose phone number is 08142/506044 looking?

   _____

8. For what starting month is the company looking for a telephone operator *(Telefonistin)*?

   _____

9. What is the German word for automobile (car) salesman?

   _____

10. In which city is a doctor's office looking for a doctor's assistant *(Arzthelferin)*?

    _____

11. A company wants to hire someone who would be able to work out of his or her home. What is this company's website address?

    _____

12. How many ads are listed here? Write the number in German.

    _____

Ausbildungsberuf **Most jobs in Germany require several years of training (*Ausbildung*) for certification. Look at the four job titles listed below.**

1. What is the length of training (*Ausbildungsdauer*) in months needed for a

   a) chemical laboratory assistant?

   _____

   b) mechanic in synthetics and rubber latex technology?

   _____

2. What is the job title of a female working in the chemical production industry?

   _____

3. What is the job title of a male working in the pharmaceutical industry?

   _____

Ausbildungsberuf	Ausbildungs-dauer in Monaten
Chemielaborant/-in	42
Chemikant/-in	36
Pharmakant/-in	36
Verfahrensmechaniker/-in für Kunststoff- und Kautschuktechnik	36

L *Ausbildung bei IGS* **Look at the ad and answer the questions.**

1. What does IGS stand for?

_____

2. In what city is the company located?

_____

Sprichwort

Erst die Arbeit, dann das Vergnügen.
Work before play.

Symtalk

M Ergänze die richtigen Wörter auf Deutsch! *(In the space, write the correct word in German.)*

1. _____

2. _____

3. _____

4. _____

5. _____

6. _____

7. _____

8. _____

N Sag die Sätze! Dann schreib sie auf Deutsch! *(Say the sentences, then write them in German.)*

1. _____

2. _____

3. _____

4.

_____

0 **Mit einem Klassenkameraden, stell die Frage oder gib die Antwort!** _(With a classmate, ask the question or give the answer. Then, write the dialogue.)_

1.

_____

2.

_____

3.

_____

4.

_____

Kreuzworträtsel

This person...

Waagerecht

2. ...brings the mail to your home.
5. ...prepares meals.
6. ...helps diagnose an ailment.
8. ...plays a musical instrument.
9. ...is someone who is in your classroom.
10. ...repairs plumbing items.

Senkrecht

1. ...performs on stage.
3. ...works with electrical wires.
4. ...makes cabinets.
7. ...paints or does sculptures.

Die Berufe

UNIT 9

Das Essen

Food

Vokabeln

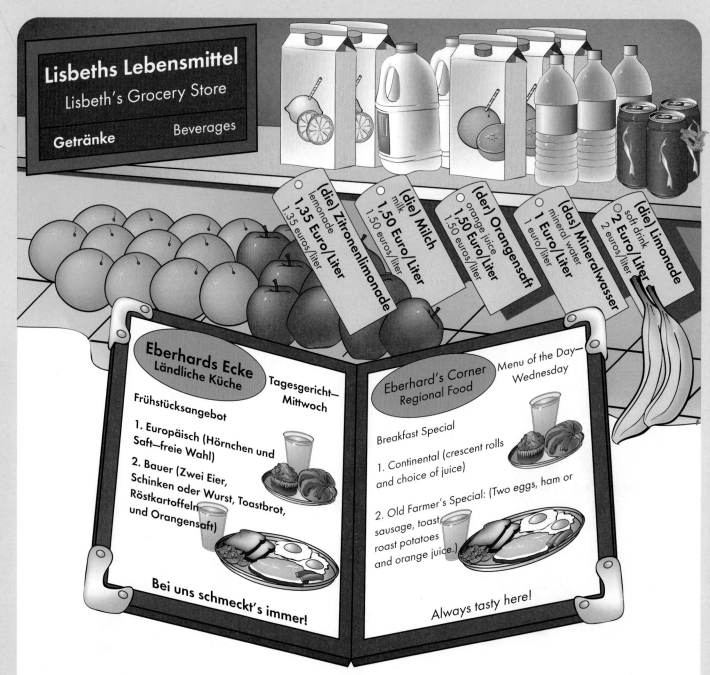

Lisbeths Lebensmittel
Lisbeth's Grocery Store

| Getränke | Beverages |

(die) Zitronenlimonade
lemonade
1,35 Euro/Liter
1.35 euros/liter

(die) Milch
milk
1,50 Euro/Liter
1.50 euros/liter

(der) Orangensaft
orange juice
1,50 Euro/Liter
1.50 euros/liter

(das) Mineralwasser
mineral water
1 Euro/Liter
1 euro/liter

(die) Limonade
soft drink
2 Euro/Liter
2 euros/liter

Eberhards Ecke
Ländliche Küche

Tagesgericht—
Mittwoch

Frühstücksangebot

1. Europäisch (Hörnchen und Saft—freie Wahl)
2. Bauer (Zwei Eier, Schinken oder Wurst, Toastbrot, Röstkartoffeln und Orangensaft)

Bei uns schmeckt's immer!

Eberhard's Corner
Regional Food

Menu of the Day—
Wednesday

Breakfast Special

1. Continental (crescent rolls and choice of juice)
2. Old Farmer's Special: (Two eggs, ham or sausage, toast, roast potatoes and orange juice.)

Always tasty here!

Was gibt's zu essen?	What's there to eat?	**Was gibt's zu trinken?**	What's there to drink?
Es gibt Suppe und Salat.	There's soup and salad.	**Es gibt Milch.**	There's milk.
Hast du Hunger?	Are you hungry?	**Hast du Durst, Ali?**	Are you thirsty, Ali?
Ja. Ich habe Hunger.	Yes. I'm hungry.	**Nein. Ich habe keinen Durst.**	No, I'm not thirsty.
Was isst du?	What are you eating?	**Was trinkst du, Matthias?**	What are you having to drink, Matthias?
Ich esse ein Butterbrot.	I'm eating a sandwich.	**Ich trinke ein Glas Milch.**	I'm having a glass of milk.

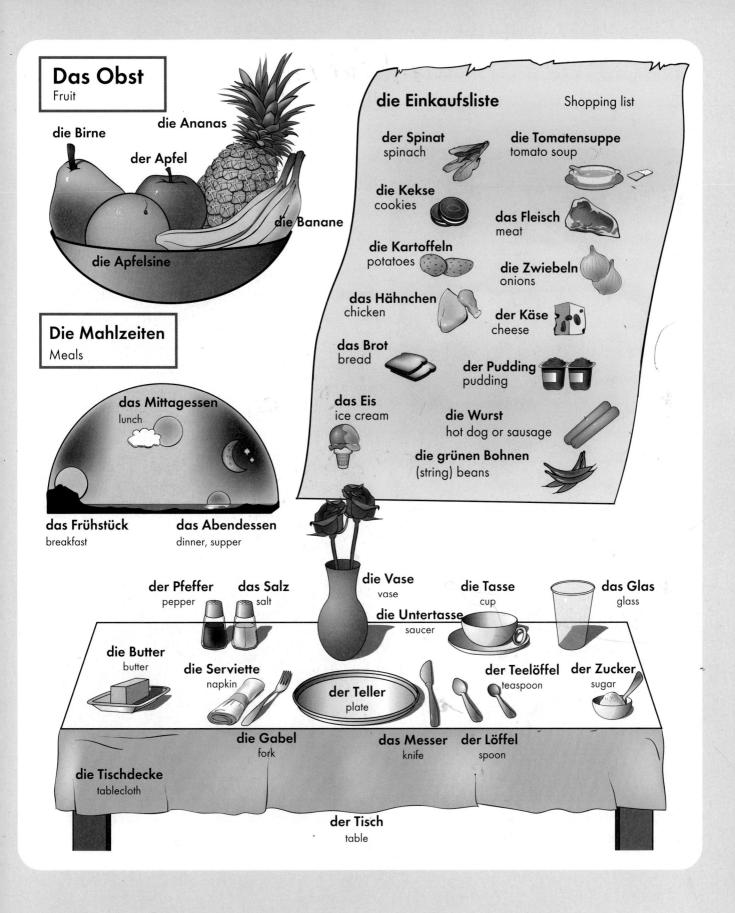

Das Obst
Fruit

die Birne

die Ananas

der Apfel

die Banane

die Apfelsine

Die Mahlzeiten
Meals

das Mittagessen
lunch

das Frühstück
breakfast

das Abendessen
dinner, supper

die Einkaufsliste
Shopping list

der Spinat
spinach

die Tomatensuppe
tomato soup

die Kekse
cookies

das Fleisch
meat

die Kartoffeln
potatoes

die Zwiebeln
onions

das Hähnchen
chicken

der Käse
cheese

das Brot
bread

der Pudding
pudding

das Eis
ice cream

die Wurst
hot dog or sausage

die grünen Bohnen
(string) beans

der Pfeffer
pepper

das Salz
salt

die Vase
vase

die Untertasse
saucer

die Tasse
cup

das Glas
glass

die Butter
butter

die Serviette
napkin

der Teller
plate

der Teelöffel
teaspoon

der Zucker
sugar

die Gabel
fork

das Messer
knife

der Löffel
spoon

die Tischdecke
tablecloth

der Tisch
table

Specialties of Germany

Schweinebraten

Schweinebraten—roast pork often served with *Semmelknödel* (Bavarian bread dumplings), applesauce, and red cabbage.

Königsberger Klopse—meatballs flavored with a sauce of cloves, peppercorns, capers and lemon juice and served with buttered noodles; specialty of *Königsberg* in the former coastal territory of East Prussia.

Strammer Max—a toasted open-face sandwich (only one slice of bread) with ham, egg, and tomatoes.

Hühnerfrikasse—a dish made with diced chicken, broth, rice, mushrooms, and peas.

Spätzle—noodles made of a flour and egg mixture dropped by a spoon into boiling water and served with butter; specialty of southwestern Germany.

Leipziger Allerlei—a dish made with all kinds *("allerlei")* of vegetables: carrots, asparagus, peas, green beans, and cauliflower. Slices of a favorite *Wurst* (sausage) can be added.

Linseneintopf—a lentil bean stew consisting of diced smoked pork, potatoes, carrots, and celery.

Lebkuchen—cookies and small cakes made of honey and spices often shaped into hearts and decorated with sayings and proverbs; specialty of Nuremberg *(Nürnberg)*.

Lebkuchen

Erdbeertorte—a sponge cake dessert made by filling the cake bottom (the *Tortenboden*) with a layer of glazed-covered strawberries. A variation is to fill it with vanilla pudding or custard and then layer with strawberries or any other fruit (*Obsttorte*).

Stollen—a holiday bread filled with raisins, chopped almonds, lemon and orange peel, and sometimes marzipan (almond paste candy). It is associated with the city of Dresden.

Stollen

- **Guten Appetit!** is a wish on the part of a friend or host for all guests to enjoy the meal and eat heartily.
- **Die Küche** can refer to the kitchen or to cooking or food in general, such as in **ländliche Küche.**
- Traditionally the large mid-day meal has several courses, often starting with soup and ending with cheese. Most people today, however, are not at home at this time. They eat out or take a bag lunch.
- Evening meals are served at a time when the whole family can sit down together.
- The noun **das Essen** means "food." The verb **essen** means "to eat."

Übungen

A Schreib den deutschen Namen von jedem Objekt! *(Write the German name of each object.)*

1. _____

2. _____

3. _____

4. _____

5. _____

6. _____

7. _____

8. _____

B Ergänze jeden Satz auf Deutsch! *(Complete each sentence in English.)*

1. *Leipziger Allerlei* is made with lots of _____.

2. *Erdbeertorte* is a sponge cake filled with _____.

3. *Strammer Max* is an open-face _____.

4. *Lebkuchen* are cookies and cake bars made with _____.

5. A *Stollen* is a holiday _____.

C Using your food vocabulary and the list of specialties, write three food items for each of the following categories.

1. **meat**
   A. _____

   B. _____

   C. _____

2. **vegetables**
   A. _____

   B. _____

   C. _____

3. **dairy products**
   A. _____

   B. _____

   C. _____

4. **beverages**
   A. _____

   B. _____

   C. _____

5. **fruits**
   A. _____

   B. _____

   C. _____

6. **desserts**
   A. _____

   B. _____

   C. _____

D Imagine you are opening a restaurant in Germany. From your food and specialty lists, prepare a menu for lunch and dinner. At least three dishes or items for each meal should be offered.

E Prepare a poster from magazine pictures. Show a balanced breakfast and a balanced dinner. Label each food item with its German name.

F Prepare fifteen different flash cards with a picture of a food item on one side and its German name on the other. Present your flash cards to the class.

G Ein Spiel (a game). Working in small groups, list (in German) twenty different foods or beverages, then scramble each word. The student who unscrambles the most words correctly will be the winner.

H Zum Sprechen. Your classmate is in charge of the menu today. In German, tell him/her that you are hungry and that you want to know what there is to eat today. Your classmate will tell you five foods. Next, he/she will tell you that he/she is thirsty and ask you what there is to drink. Answer accordingly with five beverage choices.

I Du bist dran! Imagine that you work at a very nice restaurant in Germany. A customer asks you about a regional specialty, such as *Leipziger Allerlei.* Explain what this specialty is and how it is made.

Sprichwort

Hunger ist der beste Koch. Hunger is the best cook.

J *Obst und Gemüse* (Fruits and Vegetables). Look at the two ads and then answer the questions. Note that the cost is listed in euro (€) and the weight is listed in grams (g) and kilograms (kg).

1. How much (in euro) does a pineapple cost?

   _____

2. What is the total weight of the oranges in the bucket?

   _____

3. What is the cost of the bucket filled with fruits?

   _____

4. How many kilograms (kg) of bananas can you buy for € 2.85?

   _____

5. Can you name the Spanish country where the tomatoes come from?

   _____

6. What is the cost of two bags *(Beutel)* of potatoes?

   _____

7. Are there more grapefruits or oranges in the bucket?

   _____

8. If 1 kg = 1000 g, which fruit in the bucket is half of the total weight?

   _____

K Can you guess what these German words mean in English?

1. frisch: _____
2. Qualität: _____
3. Preis: _____
4. Liter: _____
5. Vitamine: _____
6. Inhalt: _____

Symtalk

L Ergänze die richtigen Wörter auf Deutsch! *(In the space, write the correct word in German.)*

1. _____ 2. _____ 3. _____ 4. _____ 5. _____ 6. _____

M Lies die Sätze! Dann schreib sie auf Deutsch! *(Read the sentences, then write them in German.)*

1. _____

2. _____

3. _____

4. _____

5. _____

N **Mit einem Klassenkameraden, stell die Frage oder gib die Antwort!** *(With a classmate, ask the question or give the answer. Then, write the dialogue.)*

1.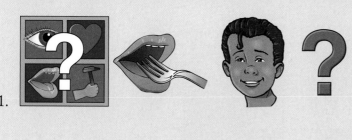

   _____

2.

   _____

3.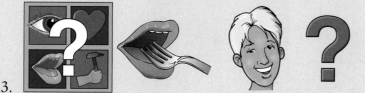

   _____

4.

   _____

5.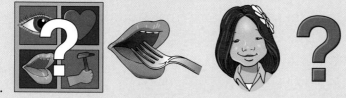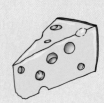

   _____

Kreuzworträtsel

Waagerecht

1. adds flavor to food
3. container to hold a beverage
6. cookies and cake bars with honey and spices
7. needed to cut food
9. *Ich habe _____.* (I'm thirsty.)
13. yellow tangy fruit
14. apples, bananas, pineapples, pears, and oranges
15. *Was gibt's zu _____?* (What is there to drink?)

Senkrecht

1. soup
2. "little cakes" or cookies
4. evening meal
5. sausage that can be sliced, served hot or cold
8. *Es gibt _____ und Suppe.*
10. needed to pick up food
11. juice from fruits or vegetables
12. *Was gibt's zu _____?* (What is there to eat?)

UNIT 10

Die Kunst

Art

Berühmte Künstler

The Young Hare

(water color, 1502) by Albrecht Dürer

Kunstverlag M.u.D. Reisser, Wien

Saint Anthony

(copper engraving, 1519) by Albrecht Dürer

Staatliche Graphische Sammlung, München

Albrecht Dürer (1471–1528) was a Renaissance artist from Nürnberg. From his study of Classical art he learned how to draw the human form realistically. He started his career by painting religious figures for altarpieces. Dürer, however, was also interested in science, proportion, and measurement. His watercolors and drawings of flowers and animals, such as *The Young Hare,* show his great interest in detail and accuracy. He created designs on wood for copper engravings. Among the most famous ones are *The Four Horsemen of the Apocalypse* and *Saint Anthony.* For a time, Dürer was the court painter of the Hapsburg Emperor.

Caspar David Friedrich (1774–1840), a North German painter from seacoast town of Greifswald, was a leading artist of the Romantic School. He did not want to imitate the classical styles of famous Italian artists. Inspired by the beauty of his homeland and by the power of nature, he created his own style. Landscapes and seascapes offered Friedrich the means to express the beauty and the

Ships in the Harbor of Greifswald

(oil on canvas, before 1810) by Caspar David Friedrich

Staaliche Museen Preußischer
Kulturbesitz, Nationalgalerie, Berlin (West)

Lone Tree

(oil on canvas, 1823)
by Caspar David Friedrich

Staaliche Museen Preußischer
Kulturbesitz, Nationalgalerie, Berlin (West)

destruction caused by nature. In the painting *Ships in the Harbor of Greifswald,* the viewer might say that the sunrise promises to drive away the gloom and the mystery of night. Or, the viewer might say that the shadows of evening threaten the peacefulness of the ships at anchor. In the *Lone Tree,* the viewer sees the effects of a violent storm (a tree hit by lightning and the water-soaked ground), while the emerging sun gradually restores the peace.

Ernst Ludwig Kirchner (1880–1938) studied art and architecture at the Dresden Technical School. He enjoyed experimenting with woodcuts and oils. He was convinced that art was being ruined by Romanticism (the Romantic School of Art) and by modern capitalistic urban society. To change this, he and his friends founded a community of artists called *Die Brücke,* or *The Bridge,* and a new style of art called Expressionism. Kirchner's painting called *Women on the Street* shows his rather negative view of society people.

Women on the Street

(oil on canvas, 1915)
by Ernst Ludwig Kirchner

Brucke Museum, Berlin, Germany

The Large Blue Horses

(oil on canvas, 1911) by Franz Marc

Collection, Walker Art Center, Minneapolis
Gift of the T. B. Walker Foundation, Gilbert M. Walker, Fund, 1942

His group gave rise to another Expressionist community in München called *Der blaue Reiter,* or *The Blue Rider.* Its style is characterized by heavy outlines, vivid colors, and simple features. *The Large Blue Horses* by **Franz Marc** is an example.

Today

Making great waves in the art world is the **New Leipzig School,** a group of artists who are combining traditional painting with new techniques. **Neo Rauch** and **Matthias Weischer** are two of its leading artists.

Germany's best known contemporary artist is **Gerhard Richter,** who was born in Dresden in 1932. He attended the Dresden Art Academy and in 1961 escaped from East Germany and settled in the city of Düsseldorf. There he continued his art studies. Richter has a wide-range of styles and subjects and often uses photographs in his creations. Many times he paints "blurry" pictures, that is, those that do not seem to be in focus. He does not believe that is possible to reproduce a picture exactly as it is in real life. Richter's paintings have been shown in museums of modern art around the world.

Jutta Votteler is well-known artist from the Rhine River area. She studied art in the city of Mainz. Specializing in colored etchings and woodcuts, this artist creates charming

Die Kunst

scenes from everyday life with just a touch of fantasy. Her delightful style focuses on puppies, cats, birds, and countless other things we see everyday.

Madeleine Dietz is a sculptor whose works combine history, religion, humanity, and ecology. The artist uses steel and concrete to represent the present cultural age, and simple earth or soil to represent nature and the past. One of her most well-known works is a simple steel box filled with dirt. She calls this her *Schatzkasten* or *"treasure chest,"* because the earth is a precious resource and should be protected. In all her sculptures she has a message for us: We learn from history and should do our best to make the world a nicer, cleaner, and more humane place to live. In tribute to her artistic achievements she was awarded the distinguished Ernst Barlach Award in 2003.

Mein kleiner Freund II
(color etching, 2001)
by Jutta Votteler

Schatzkasten
(steel and soil sculpture, 1998)
by Madeleine Dietz

Übungen

A Name the picture that shows what is described.

1. a shepherd leaning against a tree

   _____

2. a medieval city

   _____

3. an animal at rest

   _____

4. animals moving

   _____

5. working people

   _____

6. well-dressed city people

   _____

B Name the artist whose works reveal the following.

1. heavy dark outlines

   _____

2. exact proportions

   _____

3. steel and earth

   _____

4. the force of nature

   _____

5. bright colors

   _____

6. real-looking people or animals

   _____

C Match column A with column B.

A	B
1. _____ Contemporary painter	A. Dürer
2. _____ Classical style painter	B. Friedrich
3. _____ Contemporary sculptor	C. Votteler
4. _____ Romantic style painter	D. Dietz
5. _____ Expressionist style painter	E. Kirchner
6. _____ Contemporary woodcutter	F. Richter

D Complete the analogies.

1. *Lone Tree*: _____ = *The Four Horsemen*: Dürer

2. Friedrich: seascapes = _____: city scene

3. Dietz: _____ = Votteler: etchings and woodcuts

4. Franz Marc: *The Blue Rider* = Kirchner: _____

5. Friedrich: Romantic style = _____: many styles

E Match the picture cue with the associated artist's name.

1. _____ Friedrich   A.

2. _____ Kirchner   B.

3. _____ Dürer   C.

F   **Which artist would most likely be. . .**

1. . . .awed by the beauty of a sun-lit meadow and a blue sky?

   _____

2. . . .annoyed that rules, clocks, and money dominate so many people?

   _____

3. . . .happy to encourage people not to litter our planet?

   _____

G   **In your opinion whose work would. . .**

1. . . .delight a group of Renaissance scholars?

   _____

2. . . .appeal to someone who likes unusual colors for ordinary objects?

   _____

3. . . .be appreciated by lovers of landscapes?

   _____

4. . . .appeal to someone who likes photography?

   _____

5. . . .appeal to animal lovers?

   _____

H   **Which of the paintings in this unit do you like best? Who painted it? State in your own words what the picture is about and why you like it.**

   _____

   _____

   _____

   _____

   _____

   _____

   _____

I **Schreib die fehlenden Namen!** *(Write the missing names.)*

1. _____ was one of the founders of *Die Brücke* or *The Bridge*.

2. _____ was a court painter of the Hapsburg Emperor.

3. _____ believed that a picture should not be too realistic.

J **Du bist dran!** Choose an object that you have learned so far in this book, for example, a rabbit. On a sheet of paper or on the chalkboard, make your rabbit in two different styles: Classical and Modern (expressionistic, abstract or unconventional). Label each as follows: *Das ist ein Kaninchen*. Let the class see and vote twice: first on the artistic style (which drawing is classical and which is modern), and second on personal preference (which one the class prefers). Announce in German that you are an artist!

Sprichwort

Die Kunst ist lang, das Leben kurz.
Art is long-lasting, but life is short.

Lebendige Sprache

⑬ Ägyptisches Museum – Bonner Sammlung von Aegyptiaca *Freier Eintritt*

Das Ägyptische Museum zeigt in seiner Dauerausstellung ›Grab, Tempel und Haus‹ die schönsten Stücke der Ägyptischen Sammlung der Universität Bonn aus einem Zeitraum von 4000 v. Chr. bis 300 n. Chr.

Regina-Pacis-Weg 7, 53113 Bonn
Tel. (02 28) 73 97 10 oder 73 75 87
www.aegyptisches-museum.uni-bonn.de
Öffnungszeiten: Di, Mi + Fr 10-14 Uhr,
Do 14-18 Uhr, erster Sa im Monat 13-17 Uhr,
Geschlossen: 15. Aug. - 15. Sep. und 15. Dez. - 15. Jan.
ÖPNV Haltestelle: Straßenbahn 16, 63, 66 Universität/Markt

⑮ Mineralogisches Museum der Universität Bonn *Freier Eintritt*

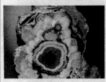

Die Dauerausstellung ›Minerale – verborgener Reichtum unseres Planeten‹ erstreckt sich über vier Säle. Besonders beliebt ist der Edelsteinsaal, in dem auch ein Einblick in die Herstellung synthetischer Kristalle gegeben wird. Das Mineralogische Museum – damals Teil eines naturhistorischen Museums – befindet sich seit 1818 im Poppelsdorfer Schloss und zählt somit zu den ältesten Museen Bonns.

Poppelsdorfer Schloss, 53115 Bonn
Tel. (02 28) 73 90 47 oder 73 27 64, www.min.uni-bonn.de
Öffnungszeiten:
Mi 15-17 Uhr, So 10-17 Uhr (außer feiertags)
ÖPNV Haltestelle: Bus vom Hbf Richtung Röttgen/Venusberg, Botanischer Garten

⑰ Schumannhaus – Musikbibliothek *Freier Eintritt*

Das Schumannhaus stammt aus der Zeit um 1790. Originalbriefe und -dokumente von Robert und Clara Schumann. Die Städtische Musikbibliothek im Haus bietet 47.000 Noten, Bücher, CDs und DVDs an. Regelmäßige Hauskonzerte.

Sebastianstraße 182, 53115 Bonn
Tel. (02 28) 77 36 56
www.schumannhaus-bonn.de

Öffnungszeiten: Mo, Mi, Do, Fr 11-13.30 Uhr und 15-18 Uhr
ÖPNV Haltestelle: Bus 622, 623, 632, 635 Alfred-Bucherer-Straße

⑱ Glasmuseum Rheinbach *Freier Eintritt*

1968 entstandenes und erstes ›Spezialmuseum für nordböhmisches Hohlglas‹. Dauerausstellung: Verschiedene Stilrichtungen der böhmischen Glasherstellung und -veredelung bis zur zeitgenössischen ›Studioglasbewegung‹.

Himmeroder Wall 6
53359 Rheinbach
Tel. (0 22 26) 92 74 10
www.glasmuseum-rheinbach.de
Öffnungszeiten: Di - Fr 10-12 Uhr und 14-17 Uhr,
Sa und So 11-17 Uhr
ÖPNV Haltestelle: DB Bahnhof Rheinbach
Bus 800 bis Hauptstraße

⑲ Stadtmuseum Siegburg *Freier Eintritt*

Auf mehr als 2000 qm wird die Geschichte Siegburgs und seiner Umgebung von der Frühzeit bis zur Gegenwart dargestellt. Schwerpunkte: Siegburger Keramik, Wechselausstellungen zeitgenössischer Kunst.

Markt 46, 53721 Siegburg
Tel. (0 22 41) 55 733
www.siegburg.de

Öffnungszeiten: Di, Mi, Fr, Sa 10-17 Uhr, Do 10-20 Uhr, So 10-18 Uhr
ÖPNV Haltestelle: U-Bahn 66 ICE-Bahnhof Siegburg

⑳ Burg Wissem – Museum der Stadt Troisdorf *Freier Eintritt*

In Europa einzigartiges Bilderbuchmuseum. Historische Kinder- und Jugendliteratur von 1498 bis in die Neuzeit, umfangreiche Sammlung von Original-Bilderbuchillustrationen, aktuelle Wechselausstellungen.

Burgallee, 53840 Troisdorf
Tel. (0 22 41) 88 41 11/-17
www.troisdorf.de
Öffnungszeiten: Di - So 11-17 Uhr
ÖPNV Haltestelle: Bf. Troisdorf, Bus 501, 506, 507, 508 Ursulaplatz/Römerstrasse

㉑ Heimatmuseum Altwindeck e. V. *Freier Eintritt*

Das alte Schulgebäude birgt seit 1974 kulturhistorisch bedeutsame Exponate. In den vergangenen Jahren wurden eine Art Freilichtmuseum mit zwei weiteren Fachwerkhäusern sowie eine Göpelmühle und eine Scheune wieder errichtet.

Im Thal Windeck, 51570 Windeck
Tel. (0 22 92) 38 88 oder 89 42
www.heimatmuseum-windeck.de
Öffnungszeiten: 1. Apr. bis 30. Nov. Sa 14-18 Uhr, So und feiertags
10-12 Uhr und 14-18 Uhr, 1. Feb. bis 31. März So und feiertags 14-18 Uhr
ÖPNV Haltestelle: U-Bahn 66 bis Siegburg, DB Siegtalstrecke RE 9
oder S12 bis Bf. Dattenfeld oder Bf. Schladern, 15 Min. Fußweg

㉒ Siebengebirgsmuseum der Stadt Königswinter *Freier Eintritt*

Ein Blick hinter die Kulissen des sagenhaften Siebengebirges – auf den Spuren von Vulkanen, Steinhauern, Romantikern, Burgen, Klöstern, Weinbau und Rheinschifffahrt. Sonderausstellungen u.a.m.

Kellerstraße 16, 53639 Königswinter
Tel. (0 22 23) 37 03
www.siebengebirgsmuseum.de

Öffnungszeiten: Täglich (außer Mo) 14-17 Uhr, Mi 14-19 Uhr,
So 11-17 Uhr, 01.11.-31.03., Mi 14-19 Uhr, Sa und So 14-17 Uhr
ÖPNV Haltestelle: U-Bahn 66 Königswinter/Fähre

K You'll notice that these descriptions are of eight different museums located in the Rhineland in the western part of Germany. Each ad has a number. Write the ad number next to each description below. Some numbers will be used more than once. This museum. . .

_____ . . . is located in Königswinter.

_____ . . . is an old school building that has housed important historical exhibits since 1974.

_____ . . . is in the *Sebastianstraße*.

_____ . . . specializes in making glass figurines.

_____ . . . contains a collection of Egyptian artifacts.

_____ . . . has the number seven in its name.

_____ . . . is located in a 2000 square meter building and exhibits ceramics and contemporary art.

_____ . . . has a collection of minerals and has been located in the Castle Poppelsdorf since 1818.

_____ . . . can be reached by taking bus number 800 to the *Hauptstraße*.

_____ . . . has historical items from the period of 4000 BC to 300 AD.

_____ . . . has original letters and documents from two famous musicians.

_____ . . . has a collection of children's and youth literature dating back to the 15th century.

L Can you guess what these words mean in English?

1. Universität: _____

2. Öffnungszeiten: _____

3. Straße: _____

4. Botanischer Garten: _____

5. Spezialmuseum: _____

6. historisch: _____

Symtalk

M Ergänze die richtigen Wörter auf Deutsch! *(In the space, write the correct word in German.)*

1. _____
2. _____
3. _____
4. _____
5. _____
6. _____
7. _____
8. _____

N Sag die Sätze! Dann schreib sie auf Deutsch! *(Say the sentences, then write them in German.)*

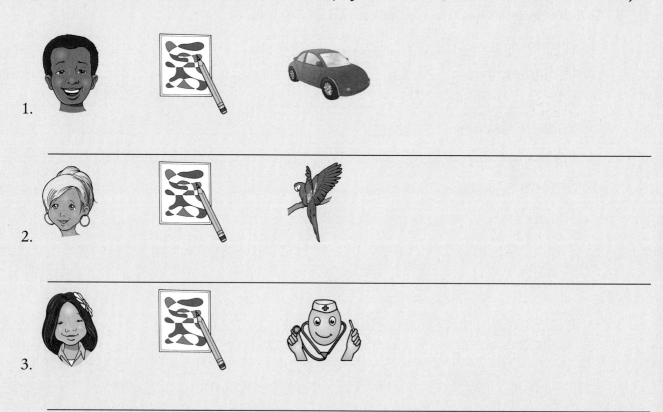

1. _____

_____

2. _____

_____

3. _____

_____

4.

_____

5.

_____

O **Mit einem Klassenkameraden, stell die Frage oder gib die Antwort!** _(With a classmate, ask the question or give the answer. Then, write the dialogue.)_

1.

_____   _____

2.

_____   _____

3.

_____   _____

4.

_____   _____

Kreuzworträtsel

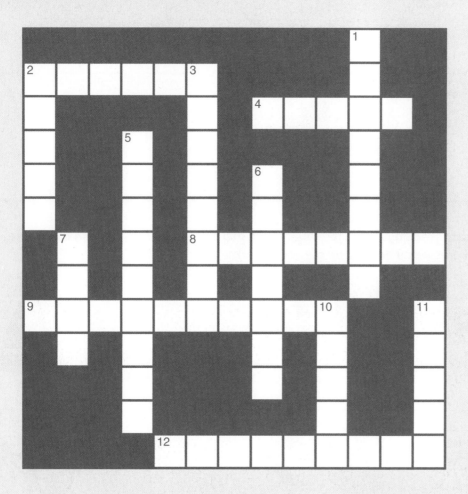

Waagerecht

2. *Die* ____ (The Bridge)
4. prize-winning sculptor
8. hometown of Dürer
9. town where Friedrich was born
12. loved the sea and the woods

Senkrecht

1. creates charming scenes
2. *Der* ____ *Reiter,* Expressionist group in München
3. one kind of work created by Votteler
5. kind of artwork created by Dürer, Friedrich, Kirchner, and Richter
6. Richter's first name
7. an Expressionist painter in München
10. died in the year 1528
11. artist associated with the New Leipzig School

UNIT 11

Der Körper und die Gesundheit
Body and Health

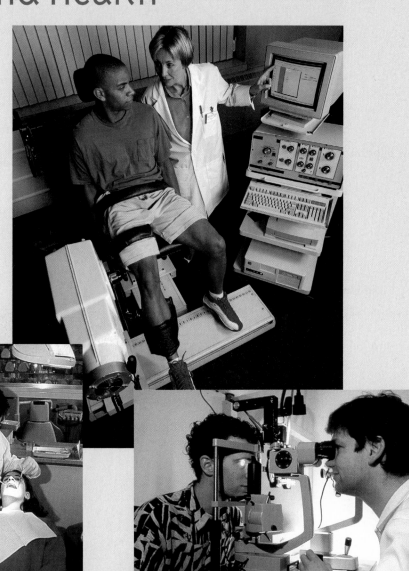

Vokabeln

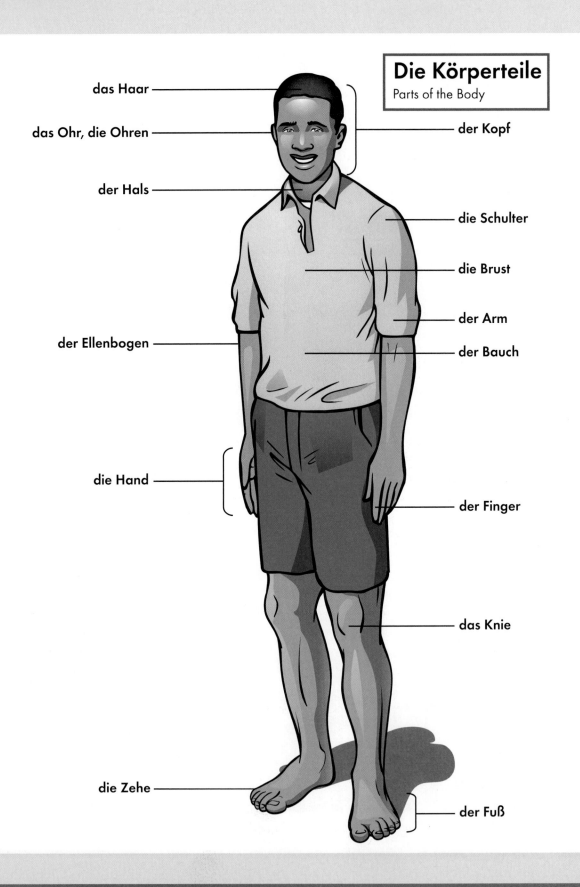

Die Körperteile
Parts of the Body

das Haar

das Ohr, die Ohren

der Hals

der Ellenbogen

die Hand

die Zehe

der Kopf

die Schulter

die Brust

der Arm

der Bauch

der Finger

das Knie

der Fuß

Die Gesichtsteile
Parts of the Face

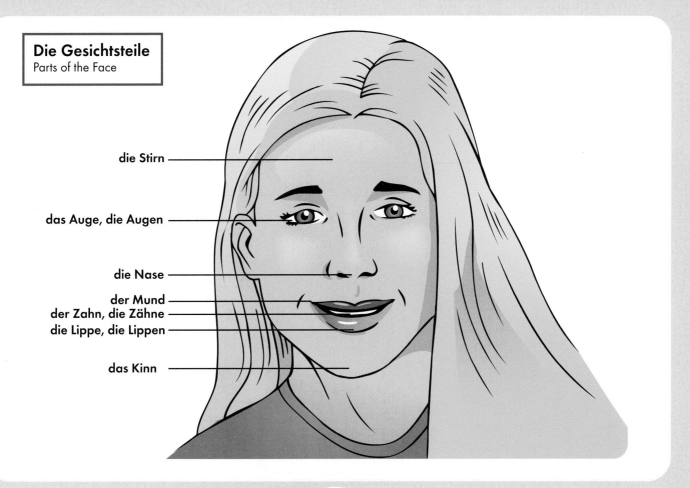

die Stirn

das Auge, die Augen

die Nase

der Mund

der Zahn, die Zähne

die Lippe, die Lippen

das Kinn

Was hast du? literally means "What do you have?" It also may refer to a problem or sickness that you may have: "What's wrong with you?"

Extra Vokabeln

die Gesundheit
health

wohl
well

glücklich
happy

krank
sick, ill

ungesund
unhealthy

gesund
healthy

traurig
sad

JASMIN: **Tag, Anja, wie geht's?**
Hi, Anja! How are you?

ANJA: **Es geht mir schlecht. Ich bin müde.**
I'm not doing well. I'm tired.

LISBETH: **Arbeitest du noch?**
Are you still working?

LUIGI: **Ja. Ich lerne für eine Klassenarbeit morgen.**
Yes. I'm studying for a test tomorrow.

HALIMA: **Was hast du?**
What is wrong with you?

AHMED: **Ich habe Kopfweh.**
I've got a headache.

KARL: **Ist Martina heute krank?**
Is Martina sick today?

STEFAN: **Ja. Sie hat die Grippe!**
Yes. She has the flu.

NELE: **Wie fühlst du dich?**
How do you feel?

MARIA: **Ich fühle mich wohl.**
I'm feeling well (not sick).

JOHANNA: **Bist du traurig, Raimund?**
Are you sad, Raimund?

RAIMUND: **Nein. Ich bin glücklich!**
No. I'm happy!

Übungen

A   **Label the parts of the body.** *(Auf Deutsch, bitte.)*

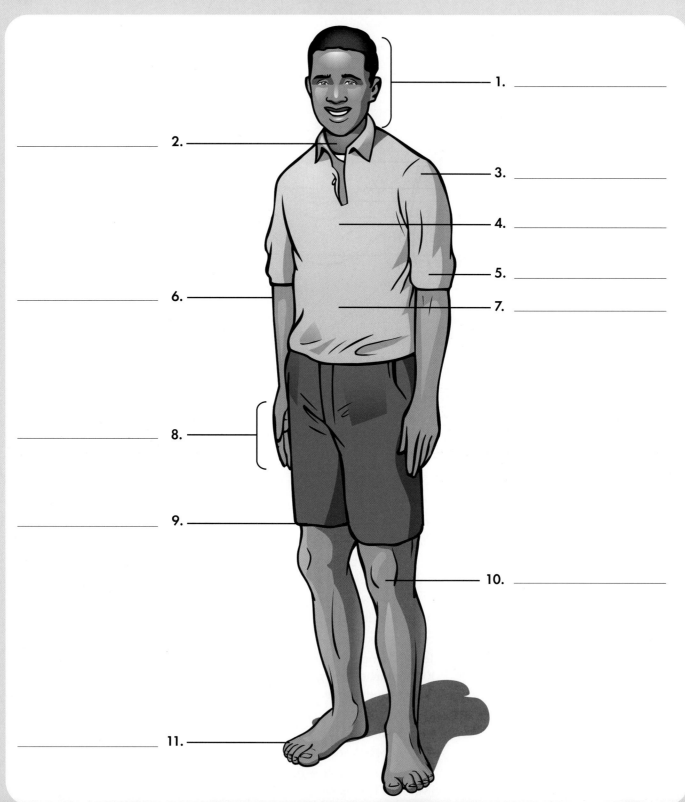

1. _____

2. _____

3. _____

4. _____

5. _____

6. _____

7. _____

8. _____

9. _____

10. _____

11. _____

B Label the parts of the face. *(Auf Deutsch, bitte.)*

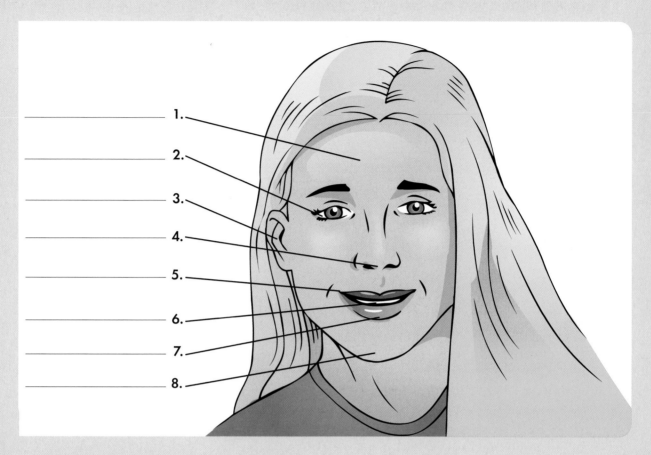

_____	1.
_____	2.
_____	3.
_____	4.
_____	5.
_____	6.
_____	7.
_____	8.

C Ergänze die Sätze auf Deutsch! *(Complete each sentence in German.)*

1. We see with our _____.

2. To speak I open my _____.

3. An _____ is necessary for hearing.

4. You hold your pen in your _____.

5. Your _____ are needed to bite and chew food.

6. One _____ has five toes.

7. We use the _____ to smell a rose.

8. We play the guitar with our _____.

9. The funny bone is located on the _____.

10. If you eat too much, your _____ will hurt.

D **What do you do with your senses? Guess the meaning of the italicized verbs. If you know the nouns, you can easily figure out the verbs!**

1. Ich *spreche* mit dem Mund. _____

2. Ich *fühle* mit den Fingern. _____

3. Ich *sehe* mit den Augen. _____

4. Ich *höre* mit den Ohren. _____

5. Ich *rieche* mit der Nase. _____

E **Ergänze die Sätze auf Deutsch!** *(Complete the sentences in German.)*

1. DIANA: Wie geht's, Ute?

    UTE: Es geht mir nicht gut. Ich fühle mich _____. *(bad, awful)*

2. DIETER: Wie geht's, Jürgen?

    JÜRGEN: Es geht mir gut. Ich fühle mich _____. *(well)*

3. DIMITRA: Hat Georg die Grippe?

    ALEXIA: Ja. Er ist _____. *(sick)*

4. BEATE: Bist du traurig?

    BENJAMIN: Nein. Ich bin _____. *(happy)*

F **Name the part of the body associated with each illustration.** *(Auf Deutsch, bitte.)*

1. _____

2. _____

3. _____

4. _____

5. _____

6. _____

7.  _____

8.  _____

9.  _____

10.  _____

G Relate each part of the body to the activity associated with it.

	A					B	
1. _____ Hand	6. _____ Bauch	A. running	F. thinking
2. _____ Fuß	7. _____ Mund	B. smelling	G. digesting
3. _____ Augen	8. _____ Arm	C. carrying	H. writing
4. _____ Nase	9. _____ Kopf	D. listening	I. touching
5. _____ Ohren	10. _____ Finger	E. seeing	J. speaking

H Lies den Absatz! *(Read the paragraph.)* Wähle die richtigen Antworten! *(Choose the correct answers.)*

> Ich heiße Alex. Ich bin vierzehn Jahre alt. Es geht mir gut und ich bin gesund. Ich *denke mit* dem Kopf. Ich spreche deutsch mit dem Mund. Ich schreibe mit der Hand und ich *gehe* mit den Beinen und Füßen zur Schule. Ich sehe die Bilder von Dürer mit den Augen. Ich *rieche* die Blumen im Garten mit der Nase. Ich esse zu Mittag mit den Zähnen. Der Körper ist fantastisch, nicht wahr?

denke	*think*	**gehe**	*walk*
mit	*with*	**rieche**	*smell*

1. Alex ist _____.
   A. ein Junge
   B. ein Mann
   C. ein Mädchen
   D. eine Frau

2. Alex ist _____ Jahre alt.
   A. 11
   B. 12
   C. 13
   D. 14

3. Alex spricht mit _____.
   A. der Hand
   B. dem Bein
   C. dem Mund
   D. dem Ohr

4. Mit den Beinen _____.
   A. geht Alex zur Schule
   B. schreibt Alex eine Postkarte
   C. spricht Alex deutsch
   D. riecht Alex die Blumen

5. Alex ist _____.
   A. traurig
   B. glücklich
   C. ungesund
   D. krank

I Zum Sprechen. **Locate ten parts of the body. Ask your classmate in German where a body part is. Your classmate will point to his/her part. Take turns until you have found and located all ten items.**

> Beispiel: A: Wo ist die Nase? *(Where is the nose?)*
> B: Hier ist die Nase. *(Here is the nose.)*

J Du bist dran! **Find magazine pictures showing healthy, active, and happy people and other pictures of people sick or looking unhappy. Paste these pictures on poster board and write a caption, that is, a short sentence about each one. For example, under a picture of a girl with a cold, write *Sie ist krank* or *Sie hat die Grippe*. Under the picture of a child playing, write *Er ist glücklich* or *Er ist gesund*.**

Lebendige Sprache

ZAHNÄRZTE

Dr. Badmann Georg und Dr. Johanna	Karlstraße 33	3802
Dr. Buchner Angelika	Bahnhofstraße 8	2030
Dr. Fischer Josef	Karlstraße 20	5272

TIERÄRZTE

Dr. Gloger-Höck Susanne/Dr. Lechner Petra	Grube 21	6279
Dr. Jobsky Edwin und Dr. Brigitte/Dr. Lehmer Johann	Am Isabellenschacht 14	3300
Marszalek Jan	Falkenstraße 1	91960

APOTHEKEN

Bahnhofsapotheke	Bahnhofstraße 21	2644
Karlapotheke	Karlstraße 12 a	1400
Kreuzapotheke	Karlstraße 33	2197
Stadtapotheke	Bahnhhofstraße 34	7020

ALLGEMEINMEDIZIN

Name	Anschrift	Telefon
Dr. Barfüßer Susanne (prakt. Ärztin)/Pschorr Walter (Arzt)	Karlstraße 7	3063
Dr. Geibel Jochen	Fischhaberstraße 1	1779
Dr. Jappe Diethard	Sigmundstraße 9 a	2617
Kirner Johann	Bahnhofstraße 21	5802

AUGENHEILKUNDE

Lenthe Hilde-Rose	Karlstraße 28	9435
Dr. Pohle Günther	Bahnhofstraße 21	2794

HALS-, NASEN- UND OHRENHEILKUNDE

Dr. Rechenauer Günter/Dr. Hack Ulrich	Karlstraße 28	1322
Dr. Riemerschmid Hartmut/Dr. Reißner Wilhelm	Karlstraße 12	3166

KINDERKRANKHEITEN

Dr. Schröder Claus-Peter	Grube 39	2029

OPTIKER

Barnikel Georg	Bahnhofstraße 16	91931
Bastian Willibald	Bahnhofstraße 28	7245
Millan Helmuth	Bahnhofstraße 40	4214

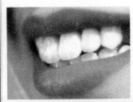

K As in all German cities and towns, there is plenty of medical assistance for the citizens in the town of Penzberg. The information given will help you answer the questions below relating to the various medical facilities. Here are a few key words that you might want to know: *Zahnarzt* = dentist, *Tierarzt* = veterinarian, *Apotheke* = pharmacy, *Allgemeinmedizin* = general medicine, *Kinderkrankheiten* = children ailments, *Optiker* = optometrist. You should be able to figure out some of the other words.

1. How many pharmacies are located on the same street? _____

2. What is Dr. Buchner's profession? _____

3. Assume that you have some eye problems and you're in the *Bahnhofstraße*. Whom should you visit? _____

4. Daniel's right ear hurts. His mother calls the pharmacy located in *Karlstraße 33*. What phone number should she dial? _____

5. Petra, who is six years old, has a stomach problem and her mother calls a doctor who exclusively treats children. Who is this doctor? _____

6. The Müllers have a dachshund that needs some medical attention. The family calls a medical office dialing the number 91960. Whose office is this? _____

7. Thomas needs new eyeglasses. He goes to Mr. Millan's eye clinic. Where is it located? _____

8. Angelika's throat is quite sore. Her mother sends her to Dr. Ulrich. However, he is not there. Who else can help her? _____

L Look at the second ad and write out at least six words that you can identify. These German words may look similar to English.

> **Beispiel**   *Privatklinik* = private clinic

1. _____   4. _____

2. _____   5. _____

3. _____   6. _____

Sprichwort

Lachen ist die beste Medizin.
Laughter is the best medicine.

Symtalk

Ergänze die richtigen Wörter auf Deutsch! *(In the space, write the correct word in German.)*

1. _____
2. _____
3. _____
4. _____
5. _____
6. _____
7. _____

Sag die Sätze! Dann schreib sie auf Deutsch! *(Say the sentences, then write them in German.)*

1. _____

2. _____

3. _____

4. _____

Der Körper und die Gesundheit

5.

_____

O **Mit einem Klassenkameraden, stell die Frage oder gib die Antwort!** *(With a classmate, ask the question or give the answer. Then, write the dialogue.)*

1.

_____

2.

_____

3.

_____

4.

_____

Kreuzworträtsel

Waagerecht

2. zum Zuhören *(listening)*
3. ____ geht's?
6. *stomach*
7. nicht krank
12. Was ____ du?
14. zum Sehen
15. Martin ist nicht traurig. Er ist ____.
17. zum Schreiben

Senkrecht

1. *flu*
4. *between shoulder and hand*
5. zum Sprechen
8. Ich fühle mich ____. *(bad)*
9. zum Riechen *(smelling)*
10. Ich habe die Grippe. Ich bin ____.
11. *well*
13. ____ ist die beste Medizin.
16. ____ habe Kopfweh.

UNIT 12

Die Kleidung

Clothing

Vokabeln

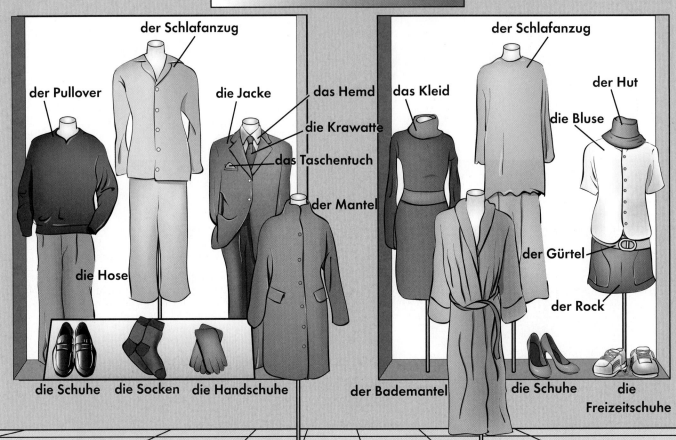

Neue Mode

der Schlafanzug

der Pullover

die Jacke

das Hemd

die Krawatte

das Taschentuch

der Mantel

die Hose

die Schuhe   die Socken   die Handschuhe

der Schlafanzug

der Hut

das Kleid

die Bluse

der Gürtel

der Rock

der Bademantel   die Schuhe   die Freizeitschuhe

HEIKE: **Was hast du an?**
What are you wearing?

RAINER: **Ich habe meinen neuen Anzug an.**
I'm wearing my new suit.

HEIKE: **Warum?**
Why?

RAINER: **Ich gehe heute Abend in ein Konzert.**
I'm going to a concert this evening.

ANDREAS: **Ich gehe draußen in den Garten.**
I'm going out into the yard.

MARIANNE: **Warte mal. Ich gehe mit. Ich hole aber zuerst meine Jacke.**
Wait for me. I'm going with you. But first I'm going to get my jacket.

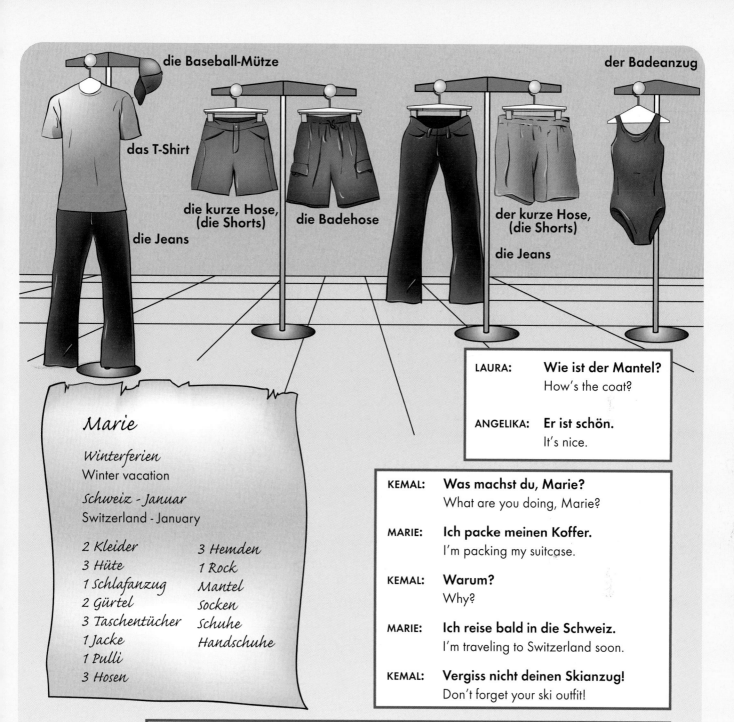

die Baseball-Mütze

der Badeanzug

das T-Shirt

die kurze Hose, (die Shorts)

die Badehose

der kurze Hose, (die Shorts)

die Jeans

die Jeans

LAURA: **Wie ist der Mantel?**
How's the coat?

ANGELIKA: **Er ist schön.**
It's nice.

KEMAL: **Was machst du, Marie?**
What are you doing, Marie?

MARIE: **Ich packe meinen Koffer.**
I'm packing my suitcase.

KEMAL: **Warum?**
Why?

MARIE: **Ich reise bald in die Schweiz.**
I'm traveling to Switzerland soon.

KEMAL: **Vergiss nicht deinen Skianzug!**
Don't forget your ski outfit!

Marie

Winterferien
Winter vacation

Schweiz - Januar
Switzerland - January

2 Kleider	*3 Hemden*
3 Hüte	*1 Rock*
1 Schlafanzug	*Mantel*
2 Gürtel	*Socken*
3 Taschentücher	*Schuhe*
1 Jacke	*Handschuhe*
1 Pulli	
3 Hosen	

- Use the pronoun *sie* to refer to a *die*-word (feminine gender word):
  Die *Krawatte ist schön.* → *Sie ist schön.*
  The necktie is nice.   It is nice.
- Use the pronoun *es* to refer to a *das*- word (neuter category word):
  Das *Kleid ist schön.* → *Es ist schön.*
- The verb "to wear" or "to have on" is *anhaben.* When you are talking about what you are wearing, be sure to place the *an* at the end of your sentence. *Ich habe die Hose an.*
- A *Pulli* is a light weight sweater, usually short sleeved. A *Pullover* is a heavier long-sleeved sweater. A *Strickjacke* is a cardigan, that is, a sweater with buttons.

Übungen

A **Welche Wörter passen zusammen?** *(Which words match?)*

A	B
1. _____ der Rock	A. handkerchief
2. _____ der Gürtel	B. jacket
3. _____ die Hose	C. coat
4. _____ die Krawatte	D. tie
5. _____ die Handschuhe	E. skirt
6. _____ das Taschentuch	F. belt
7. _____ der Bademantel	G. pants
8. _____ der Mantel	H. shoes
9. _____ die Schuhe	I. gloves
10. _____ die Jacke	J. bathrobe
11. _____ der Badeanzug	K. baseball cap
12. _____ die Baseball-Mütze	L. bathing suit

B **Was hast du an . . . ?** *(What do you wear . . . ?)* **Auf Deutsch, bitte.**

1. . . . to school?

_____

2. . . . to a symphony concert?

_____

3. . . . to bed?

_____

4. . . . in cool weather?

_____

5. . . . in cold weather?

_____

C **Complete the analogies.**

1. Krawatte: _____ = Gürtel: Hose

2. Bademantel: Schlafanzug = Mantel: _____

3. Handschuhe: Hände = _____: Füße

4. _____: Rock = Hemd: Hose

D **Ergänze jeden Satz mit dem deutschen Wort zu jeder Abbildung!** *(Complete each sentence with the German word for the illustration.)*

1. Heike hat ein _____ an.

2. Thomas hat einen _____ an.

3. Ali hat einen _____ an.

4.

Maria hat einen _____

und eine _____ an.

5.

Christian hat ein _____

und eine _____ an.

E **Schreib die Wörter auf Englisch!** *(Write the words in English.)*

1. anhaben = to _____

2. er/sie hat an = _____

3. ich habe an = _____

4. du hast an = _____

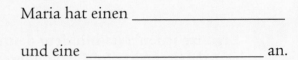

Was haben sie an?

F List the required number of items for each category. *Auf Deutsch, bitte.*

outdoor clothing (4)

1. _____

2. _____

3. _____

4. _____

accessories (3)

5. _____

6. _____

7. _____

footwear (3)

8. _____

9. _____

10. _____

sleepwear (1)

11. _____

G Wähle das richtige Wort, um jeden Satz zu vollenden! *(Choose the correct word in order to complete each sentence.)*

1. Ich packe meinen _____.
   A. Koffer
   B. Kartoffeln
   C. Küche
   D. Konzert

2. Was hast du an?
   A. Taschentücher
   B. Abend
   C. Januar
   D. Hose

3. Vergiss nicht deinen _____!
   A. Skianzug
   B. Garten
   C. Schweiz
   D. Zürich

4. Warum holst du eine Jacke?
   A. Warte mal!
   B. Ich gehe in den Garten.
   C. Das ist meine Krawatte.
   D. Ich habe einen Koffer.

5. Warum hast du ein neues Kleid an?
   A. Ich reise in die Schweiz.
   B. Ich gehe in den Garten.
   C. Ich gehe in ein Konzert.
   D. Ich packe meine Kleidung.

6. Wie ist das Kleid?
   A. zuerst
   B. anhaben
   C. packe
   D. schön

Lies den Abschnitt! Wähle die richtigen Antworten. *(Read the paragraph. Select the correct answers.)*

> Marie *geht* mit ihrer Familie *in den Urlaub.* Sie reist nach Zürich, einer *Stadt* in der Schweiz. Sie packt ihren Koffer nur mit ihrer Winterkleidung. Sie *wählt:* zwei Hosen, zwei Pullover, ein Kleid, einen Rock, eine Bluse und eine Jacke. Sie hat alle *nötigen Kleidungsstücke* für *ihren* Urlaub in der Schweiz.

geht. . . in den Urlaub	*goes on vacation*
Stadt	*city*
wählt	*chooses*
nötigen	*necessary*
Kleidungsstücke	*articles of clothing*
ihren	*her*

1. Wer geht in den Urlaub?
   A. Urlaub
   B. Zürich
   C. Schweiz
   D. Marie

2. Was ist in dem Koffer?
   A. die Schweiz
   B. die Familie
   C. der Urlaub
   D. die Winterkleidung

3. Wie viele Hosen wählt sie? *(What does she choose?)*
   A. vier
   B. drei
   C. zwei
   D. eine

4. Packt sie eine Jacke in ihren Koffer?
   A. Ja, sie packt eine Jacke.
   B. Nein, sie packt zwei Jacken.
   C. Nein, sie packt drei Jacken.
   B. Nein, sie packt vier Jacken.

Was kann man hier kaufen?
(What can you buy here?)

I In your opinion, what other articles of clothing should Marie take along for the cold winter days of January in Switzerland? Answer in German.

_____

_____

_____

_____

_____

J **Zum Sprechen.** Ask your speaking partner what he/she is wearing today? *"Was hast du heute an?"* He/she should answer with: *Ich habe _____ an*, naming an article of clothing. Then reverse roles. Be sure to mention at least three items each.

K **Du bist dran!** Time yourselves for this one. Set a stopwatch for twenty seconds. Your partner will randomly select a category of clothing, for example, indoor casual clothing. If you can say correctly all the items appropriate to that category, give yourself a gold star. If you can't, or if the clock beats you, your partner takes over. This time, you select a category, and he/she will answer. Continue until all of the categories are covered: indoor casual clothes, outdoor cold weather clothes, bedtime clothes, accessories, and special occasion clothing. The person with more gold stars wins.

Sprichwort

Das Hemd ist mir näher als der Rock.*
Blood is thicker than water.

*In the 18th century, a *Rock* was a dress coat worn by a soldier or a forester. The literal translation of this old saying is: "The shirt is closer than the coat."

Lebendige Sprache

Herren-Cargo-Hosen je **9.-**

Herren-Anzug mit Weste **49.-**

SHAMP®
T-Shirt für Damen und Herren
Basic-T-Shirt „American Style"

In modischen Farben, Rundhals-ausschnitt mit Lycra-verstärktem Stehbündchen, ohne Seitennaht, Uni-Farben: **reine super-gekämmte Baumwolle**, Melangefarben: Baumwolle/ViskoseMischung, versch. Farben, Größen: S - XXL

Farb-beispiel

Stück **1,99***

Herren-Baseball-Caps je **3.-**

SHAMP®
Walking-/Runningschuhe
für Damen und Herren.

Farb-beispiele

je Paar **13,99***

Aus weichem Synthetikmaterial kombiniert mit Nylon-Mesh, mit schweißaufsaugendem Textil-Innenfutter, herausnehmbare Einlege-sohle mit Textil bezogen und Gelkissen aus Technogel in der Ferse und im Vorderfußbereich, in versch. Farbstellungen und Größen

SHAMP®
Sport-T-Shirt
für Damen und Herren

Funktionelles Sport-T-Shirt für optimales Körperklima, weich, hautsympatisch und formstabil, bequemer Schnitt für optimale Bewegungsfreiheit, bestehend aus 100% Polyester, in versch. Farben und Modellen, Größen: S -XL

Modell-beispiele

Stück **4,99***

Stück **3,99***

ENRICO MORI®
Herren-Polohemd

Farb-beispiel

60% Baumwolle und 40% Polyester, in aktuellen Farben, Größen: M - XXL (48/50 - 58)

Dessin-beispiel

Stück **7,99***

CAMARGUE®
Herren-Oberhemd

Hochwertiges Langarmhemd aus **reiner Baumwolle**, pflege- und bügelleicht, Kent- oder Button-Down-Kragenform, in den Unifarben: Weiß, Beige und Blau oder buntgewebt in modischen Karo- oder Streifen-dessins, Größen: 40 - 45

Farb-beispiel

Stück **3,49***

SHAMP®
Modisches Herren-T-Shirt

Frontdruck und z. T. Druck auf dem Rückenteil, **reine Baumwolle**, in aktuellen Farben, Größen: M - XXL

L **Look at the clothing ads and then answer the questions.**

1. How many *Herren-Baseball-Caps* are there? *(Auf Deutsch, bitte!)*

   _____

2. What is 40% of the material in the *Herren-Polohemd?*

   _____

3. How much (in euros) would it cost to buy three *"American Style" T-Shirts* either for men or women?

   _____

4. Are the *Walking-/Runningschuhe* only for men?

   _____

5. How many pieces are there in the *Herrenanzug?* Name them. *(Auf Deutsch, bitte!)*

   _____

6. How many *Herren-Cargo-Hosen* could you buy for 45 euros?

   _____

7. What is the German word for "sizes?"

   _____

8. What is the cost of the *T-Shirt* with the widest range of sizes? What are the sizes available?

   _____

9. In which sizes is the *Herren-Oberhemd* available?

   _____

10. Can you figure out the German word for "color" or "colors"?

   _____

M **If you had enough money, which of the clothing items shown would you buy? Give three reasons.**

_____

_____

_____

_____

_____

Symtalk

N   **Ergänze die richtigen Wörter auf Deutsch!** *(In the space, write the correct word in German.)*

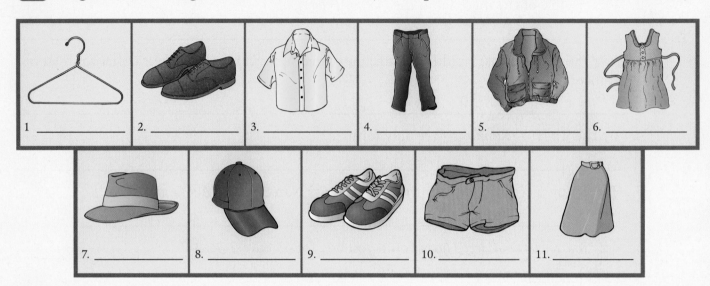

1. _____
2. _____
3. _____
4. _____
5. _____
6. _____
7. _____
8. _____
9. _____
10. _____
11. _____

O   **Sag die Sätze! Dann schreib sie auf Deutsch!** *(Say the sentences, then write them in German.)*

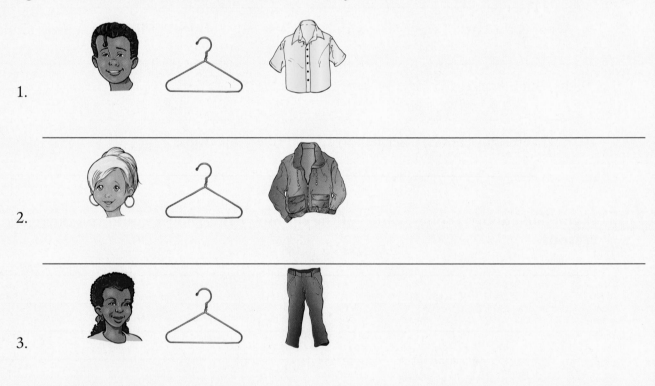

1. _____

2. _____

3. _____
   _____

4.

_____

P **Mit einem Klassenkameraden, stell die Frage oder gib die Antwort!** *(With a classmate, ask the question or give the answer. Then, write the dialogue.)*

1.

Nein, _____

_____   _____

2.

Nein, _____

_____   _____

3.

Nein, _____

_____   _____

4.

Nein, _____

_____   _____

Kreuzworträtsel

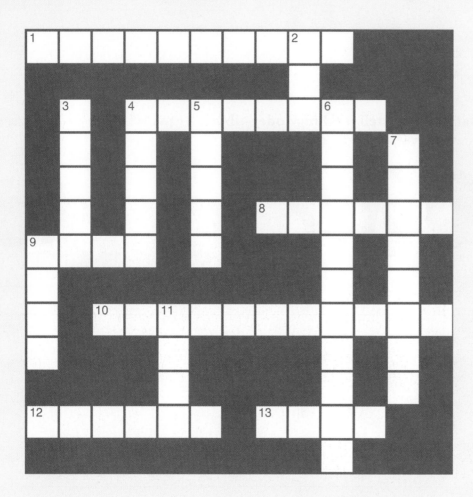

Waagerecht

1. hand protectors
4. boy's formal shirt accessory
8. first thing you put on your feet
9. *Das _____ ist mir näher als der Rock.*
10. outfit for sleeping
12. secures pants/trousers
13. usually worn with a blouse

Senkrecht

2. headgear
3. short lightweight coat
4. dressy garment for a girl
5. man's matching pants, jacket and vest
6. a pocket accessory
7. includes all articles of clothing
9. pair of pants or trousers
11. *Ich _____ einen Mantel an.*

Unit 13

Die Zeit und die Farben
Time and Colors

Vokabeln

Wie viel Uhr ist es?
What time is it?

Es ist halb zwei.   **Es ist drei Uhr.**   **Es ist Viertel vor zehn.**   **Es ist Mittag.**

Um wie viel Uhr . . . ?
At what time . . . ?

Es ist fünf nach zwei.   **Es ist Viertel nach sieben.**   **Es ist fünf vor zwölf.**   **Es ist Mitternacht.**

- Transportation in Europe operates on official time, which is on a twenty-four hour basis. Official time is often used by school, radio and television stations, and theaters. (Keep on counting after 12 noon: 13 *Uhr* = 1 p.m. etc. until 24 *Uhr* = 12 midnight.)

- *die Stunde* = the hour; *die Stunden* = the hours

- *die Uhr* = clock. *Wie viel Uhr ist es?* literally means "how much (of the) clock is it?"

- The number **eins** (one) becomes **ein** in expressions of time: **Es ist ein Uhr** (1:00).

- **Es ist halb zwei** means the hour hand is half way to two, that is, one-thirty.

- **vor** = before; **nach** = after

Welche Farbe hat. . .?
What color is. . .?

Welche Farbe(n) haben. . .?
What color(s) are. . .?

Er ist. . ./Sie ist. . ./Es ist. . .
It is. . .

Sie sind. . .
They are. . .

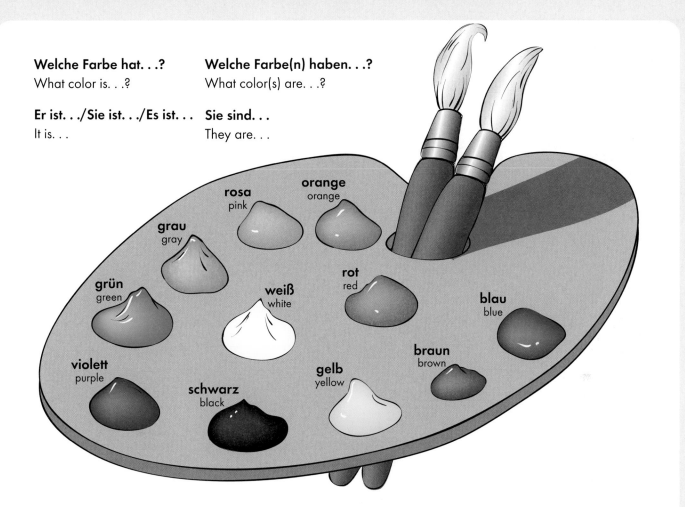

rosa
pink

orange
orange

grau
gray

grün
green

weiß
white

rot
red

blau
blue

violett
purple

schwarz
black

gelb
yellow

braun
brown

Fatima:	Welche Farbe hat **das Gras?** (grass)**?**
Jasmin:	Es ist grün.
Jochen:	Welche Farbe haben die Tomaten?
Jens:	Sie sind rot.

A **Listen as your teacher indicates a time. Find the clock which expresses that time. Mark the clock expressing the time said first with the number one. Mark the clock expressing the time said next with the number two. Continue numbering until all eight clocks are found and marked.**

1. _____

2. _____

3. _____

4. _____

5. _____

6. _____

7. _____

8. _____

B **Ergänze die Sätze auf Deutsch!** *(Complete the sentences in German.)*

1. Light red is called _____.

2. A bluebird or robin's egg is _____.

3. A piece of chocolate is _____.

4. Lemons and dandelions are _____.

5. A leaf in the summer is _____.

6. A typical ant is _____.

7. A fruit gives its name to the _____ color.

8. The sky on a very cloudy or overcast day appears _____.

9. A marshmallow is _____.

10. The color of a strawberry is _____.

C **Schreib auf Deutsch!** *(Write in German.)*

1. At seven o'clock. . .

   _____

2. It's half past one.

   _____

3. At 8:10. . .

   _____

4. It's 2:40.

   _____

5. At twenty after three. . .

   _____

Welche Farben haben sie? *(What colors are they?)* **Match the items in column *A* with the colors in column *B*.**

A   B

1. _____

A. gelb

2. _____

B. grau

3. _____

C. blau

4. _____

D. rot

5. _____

E. grün

E **Beantworte mit *ja* oder *nein*! (Answer with "yes" or "no.")**

1. Ist das Gras grün? _____

2. Sind Tomaten blau? _____

3. Ist der Elefant gelb? _____

4. Sind die Bananen orange? _____

5. Ist der Apfel rot? _____

Welche Farben haben die Äpfel?

Lies den Absatz! Wähle die richtigen Antworten! *(Read the passage. Choose the correct answers.)*

> Torsten geht *mit seiner Freundin* Karina *ins Kino*. Der Film beginnt um acht Uhr am Abend. Torsten hat seinen neuen blauen Anzug, ein weißes Hemd und eine rote Krawatte an. Karina hat eine gelbe Bluse, gelbe Socken und einen grünen Rock an. *Die beiden Freunde* haben schwarze Schuhe an. Es ist *jetzt* Viertel nach sieben und Torsten geht *zu* Karinas Haus.

mit seiner Freundin	with his girlfriend
ins Kino	to the movies
die beiden Freunde	both friends
jetzt	now
zu	to

1. **Wer ist Karina?**
   A. die Mutter von Torsten
   B. die Tante von Torsten
   C. die Freundin von Torsten
   D. die Kusine von Torsten

2. **Wohin gehen Torsten und Karina?**
   (Where do they go?)
   A   aufs Land
   B. ins Restaurant
   C. ins Kino
   D. in den Park

3. **Welche Farbe hat Torstens Krawatte?**
   A. grün
   B. rot
   C. blau
   D. weiß

4. **Welche Farbe haben Karinas Socken?**
   A. gelb
   B. braun
   C. schwarz
   D. grau

5. **Um wie viel Uhr geht Torsten zu Karinas Haus?**
   A. um 7.15 Uhr
   B. um 6.45 Uhr
   C. um 6.30 Uhr
   D. um 8.00 Uhr

6. **Um wie viel Uhr beginnt der Film?**
   A. um sieben Uhr
   B. um Viertel nach sieben
   C. um acht Uhr
   D. um halb neun

Color the clock according to the directions.

Es ist 9 Uhr.

Die Zeit und die Farben

1. die Nase: gelb
2. die Augen: blau
3. das Haar: grün
4. das Gesicht: orange
5. der Mund: braun
6. die Schuhe: grau

7. die Zahl **vier:** schwarz
8. die Zahl **sechs:** violett
9. die Zahl **drei:** rot
10. der Buchstabe *(letter)* **E:** weiß
11. der Buchstabe **i:** rosa
12. der Buchstabe **U:** schwarz

H **Zum Sprechen.** **You want to know at what time certain things take place:** *die Deutschstunde* (German class)**,** *das Konzert* **and** *das Picknick.* **Start with:** *Um wie viel Uhr ist ____?* **Your speaking partner should answer you by mentioning a specific time of day or evening.**

I *Begrüßungen.* **Your speaking partner will give you 6 times of day in German. In response to each, say an appropriate greeting:** *Guten Tag, Guten Abend, Gute Nacht.* **When you have finished, reverse the roles.**

J **Du bist dran!** **One of your classmates acts as quizmaster and the other classmates will answer. Walk around your room and point to an object. Ask,** *"Welche Farbe hat das?"* **Your classmate will answer** *"Das ist ____,"* **naming the correct color. If someone answers incorrectly, he/she drops out of the contest. Keep going, pointing to different objects, until you have just one classmate left. That person is the winner. The quizmaster determines if answers are correct.**

Sprichwort

Besser spät als nie.
Better late than never.

Lebendige Sprache

ARD ①

5.30 Morgenmagazin 9.00 heute 9.05 Happy Birthday 9.55 Wetter 10.00 heute 10.03 Brisant 10.30 Zwei am großen See – Feindliche Übernahme. TV-Heimatkomödie, D 2006 12.00 heute mittag 12.15 ARD-Buffet. Hallo Buffet (Call-In): Rechte des Vermieters – wenn der Mieter nicht zahlt / Teledoktor: Lärm & Bluthochdruck 13.00 Mittagsmagazin
14.00 Tagesschau
14.10 ② ◑ In aller Freundschaft
15.00 Tagesschau
15.10 ◑ Sturm der Liebe
16.00 ② Tagesschau
16.10 ◑ Panda, Gorilla & Co. Doku-Soap
17.00 ② Tagesschau
17.15 Brisant
17.47 Tagesschau

ZDF

5.30 Morgenmagazin 9.00 heute 9.05 Volle Kanne – Service täglich. U.a.: Top-Thema: Kinderängste / Grüne' Spargelrahmsuppe mit Frischkäse-Räucherlachs / Teckel aus Tecklenburg / Richtig eingekauft und Geld gespart 10.30 Julia – Wege zum Glück 11.15 Reich und schön 12.00 heute mittag 12.15 drehscheibe Deutschland 13.00 Mittagsmagazin
14.00 ◑ heute – in Deutschland
14.15 ◑ Tessa – Leben für die Liebe
15.00 ◑ heute – Sport
15.15 16:9 ◑ Tierisch Kölsch
16.00 ◑ heute – in Europa
16.15 ② ◑ Julia
17.00 ② ◑ heute – Wetter
17.15 ◑ hallo Deutschland
17.45 ◑ Leute heute

NDR

6.50 Vor 20 Jahren 7.05 Tutenstein 7.30 Sesamstraße 8.00 mare-TV 8.10 Sturm der Liebe 9.00 Nordmagazin 9.30 Hamburg Journal 10.00 S-H-Magazin 10.30 buten un binnen 11.00 Hallo Niedersachsen 11.30 Wildnis Mississippi – Leben am großen Fluss 12.15 Lindenstraße 12.45 Schätze der Welt 13.00 SOS – Haus & Garten 13.30 Brisant
14.00 ◑ DAS! ab 2 Frauenboxen
14.30 ◑ Bilderbuch Deutschland
15.15 ◑ Das Kinderparlament von Rajasthan
16.00 DAS! ab 4 Gast: Ali Wichmann (Firmen-Theater) / Koch: Alexander Tschebull
18.00 ◑ Hallo Niedersachsen

Ribnitz-Damgarten

Schwerin

Schönberg

Barth

Krakow am See

Stralsund

K *Um wie viel Uhr beginnt das Programm. . .?* Three of Germany's major television channels (ARD, ZDF, and NDR) offer various programs throughout the day. Indicate the time and on which channel each of the following programs begins. *Auf Deutsch, bitte!*

> **Beispiel:** Reich und schön
> Das Programm *Reich und schön* beginnt im ZDF
> um Viertel nach elf.

1. Das Programm *Hallo Niedersachsen* beginnt _____.
   _____.

2. Das Programm *Julia* beginnt am Nachmittag *(afternoon)* _____.
   _____.

3. Das Programm *Lindenstraße* beginnt _____.
   _____.

4. Das Programm *Volle Kanne* beginnt _____.
   _____.

5. Das Programm *Mittagsmagazin* beginnt _____.
   _____.

6. Das Programm *Tagesschau* beginnt am Abend *(evening)* _____.
   _____.

7. Das Programm *heute – Wetter* beginnt am Abend _____.
   _____.

8. Das Programm *Vor zwanzig Jahren* beginnt _____.
   _____.

L The following are some of the coats of arms of German towns and cities. Look at each and write the colors that you see in the coat of arms for each city listed.

1. Schönberg: _____
2. Schwerin: _____
3. Stralsund: _____
4. Krakow am See: _____
5. Ribnitz-Damgarten: _____
6. Barth: _____

Symtalk

M **Ergänze die richtigen Wörter auf Deutsch!** *(In the space, write the correct word in German.)*

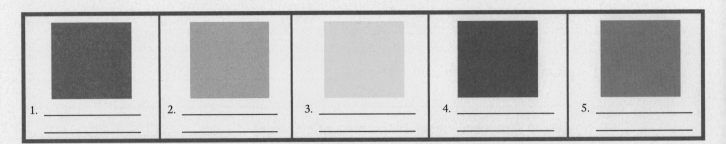

1. _____
2. _____
3. _____
4. _____
5. _____

N **Sag die Sätze! Dann schreib sie auf Deutsch!** *(Say the sentences, then write them in German.)*

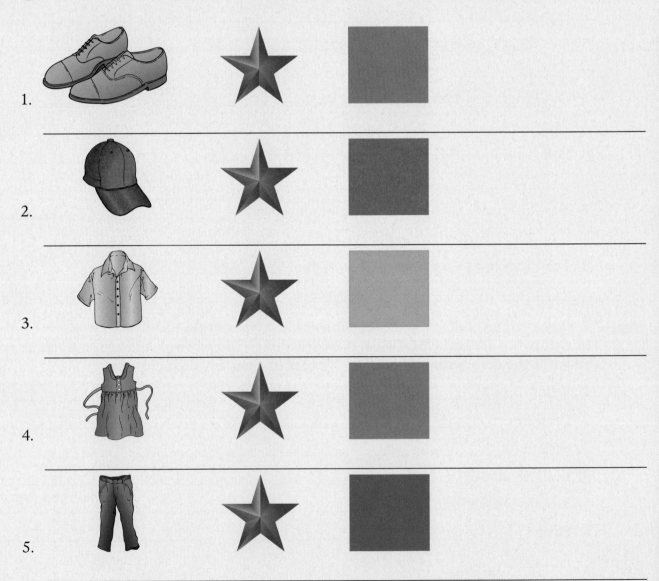

1. _____

2. _____

3. _____

4. _____

5. _____

O **Mit einem Klassenkameraden, stell die Frage oder gib die Antwort!** *(With a classmate, ask the question or give the answer. Then, write the dialogue.)*

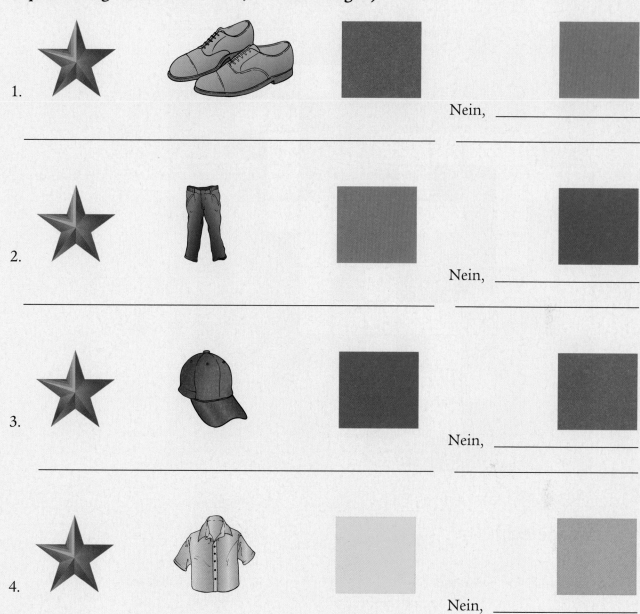

1.

_____ Nein, _____

_____

2.

_____ Nein, _____

_____

3.

_____ Nein, _____

_____

4.

_____ Nein, _____

_____

Kreuzworträtsel

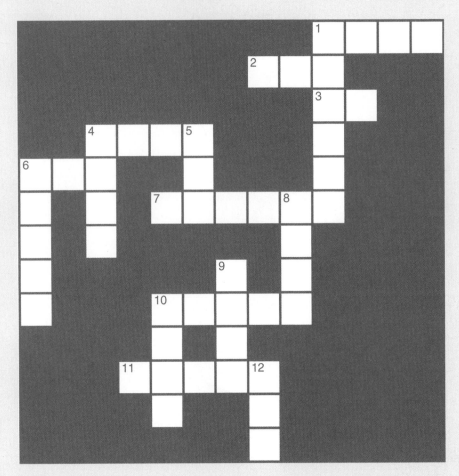

Note: ß = SS

Waagerecht

1. Besser _____ als nie.
2. Farbe von Tomaten
3. _____ wie viel Uhr beginnt der Film?
4. Farbe von Elefanten
6. _____ viel Uhr ist es?
7. Farbe von Apfelsinen
10. Farbe von Schokolade *(chocolate)*
11. Welche _____ hat das Gras?

Senkrecht

1. 60 Minuten
4. Farbe von Butter
5. Wie viel _____ ist es?
6. Farbe von Milch
8. Farbe von Gras
9. Es ist _____ neun. *(8:30)*
10. Farbe von Blaubeeren *(blueberries)*
12. Es ist _____ Uhr. *(1:00)*

UNIT 14

Die Musik

Music

Aus dem Programm
Mai – Oktober

Wolfgang Amadeus Mozart
Serenade
»Eine kleine Nachtmusik«

Orchesterkonzert
für Violine, Klarinette oder Klavier

Arien
Sinfonien
Divertimenti

Johann Strauß
Walzer
&
Polka
*Mozart Kammerorchester
Salzburg*
Mozart Chamber Orchestra Salzburg

W. A. Mozart

Johann Strauß

Berühmte Musiker

Johann Sebastian Bach
1685–1750

Johann Sebastian Bach (1685–1750) was born in Eisenach. Orphaned at the age of ten and raised by his brother, young Bach was a gifted musician. He played the harpsichord, the organ, and the violin expertly and, in addition, wrote hundreds of musical compositions. He specialized in church music (such as *cantatas*), fugues for the keyboard, and works for individual and group instruments. His longest employment was as organist and choir teacher at St. Thomas Church in Leipzig. Today Bach is considered a major composer and the father of Baroque style of music. Unfortunately, his poor eyesight and the strain from writing so much music led to total blindness. The *Six Brandenburg Concertos* and the choral works *St. Matthew Passion* and *The Mass in B Minor* are some of his outstanding creations.

Wolfgang Amadeus Mozart (1756–1791) was born in Salzburg, Austria. He was educated by his father, an accomplished musician, and wrote minuets at the age of five. At six, he performed as a child star at the royal courts of Europe. As a young man, he became the finest representative of the Classical period of music. Mozart's fame resided in his ability to learn, reproduce from memory, and create masterpieces effortlessly. He wrote over 600 compositions, including 41 symphonies, chamber music, church music, operas, and sonatas for piano and violin.

Wolfgang Amadeus Mozart
1756–1791

In spite of his superb talent, Mozart was paid poorly. He never earned enough to support his family and, eventually, poor health and circumstances led to his early death. He caught the disease typhus and died at age 35. His masterpieces include *Eine Kleine Nachtmusik* (chamber music), *Die Zauberflöte* (*The Magic Flute*, opera), and the *Jupiter Symphony*.

Ludwig van Beethoven
1770–1827

Ludwig van Beethoven (1770–1827) was born in Bonn, a village on the Rhine River. He was introduced to music at an early age and soon became an organist at the Elector's court. Beethoven traveled to Vienna, the musical capital of Europe at the time, but had to go back to Bonn because of family problems. Once back in Vienna, he studied music (for a short time under Haydn) and established himself as an independent composer.

Living at the time of the French Revolution, Beethoven became interested in the democratic ideals of equality and freedom from tyranny. He also shared the Romantic artists' views of nature and beauty. Many of his musical works reflect these interests: the opera *Fidelio,* the Moonlight Sonata and the 5th and 6th Symphonies. The 6th Symphony is called *The Pastoral* because it suggests a country atmosphere. Many personal problems, including the custody of a nephew, caused unhappiness for this gifted musician. Increasing hearing loss led to twelve years of deafness. Today Beethoven is considered the greatest composer of the Romantic Age of Music.

Contemporary Musicians

Contemporary rock music in Europe has been greatly influenced by the English-speaking world of jazz, rock and roll, the blues, country western, and progressive rock. Many German bands lean heavily on these models, while others create their own unique styles. The following groups incorporate a variety of styles such as rap and soul and many now sing in German as well as English: Among the older groups are **Kraftwerk, die Prinzen, Rammstein,** and **die Dissidenten.** (**Die Dissidenten** also sing in different languages and play the instruments of ethnic cultures in an effort to unite the world through music.) There are dozens of newer bands such as the **Wise Guys, Wir sind die Helden, die Fantastischen Vier, Fettes Brot** and **Sportfreunde Stiller.** Two all female bands are **Tic-tac-toe** and **Samojona. Clepsydra** is a band from Switzerland. Some recent bands sing only in German: **Rosenstolz, Silbermond, 2raumwohnung** and **Juli.**

Eva Briegel of Juli

Xavier Naidoo

In terms of popular singers, **Herbert Grönemeyer** and **Reinhard Mey** are legendary superstar songwriters and performers. Individuals with more traditional singing styles include **Peter Licht, Nena, Uwe Jensen, Stefanie Hertl, Matthias Reim** and **Anja Regitz.** Other singers such as **Blümchen, Clueso, Xavier Naidoo,** and **Joachim Witt** entertain generally with a variety of rock, rap and electronic sounds. **Sabine Neibersch** and **Christina Stürmer** are popular Austrian singers. In terms of classical music, the superstar is singer **Thomas Quasthoff,** a bass/baritone who gives outstanding interpretations of songs by Schubert, Brahms, and Liszt.

Übungen

A **Give the full name of the composer who did the following:**

1. effortlessly memorized and played music

   _____

2. composed for church services and individual instruments

   _____

3. started his career as an organist at the Elector's court

   _____

B **Match column *A* with column *B*.**

A	B
1. _____ *Jupiter Symphony*	A. symphony by Beethoven
2. _____ *Brandenburg Concertos*	B. where Bach lived
3. _____ *The Pastoral*	C. masterpiece by Mozart
4. _____ Salzburg	D. instrumental works by Bach
5. _____ Leipzig	E. birthplace of Mozart

C **Guess who. . .**

1. . . . was a child-star.

   _____

2. . . . worked at St. Thomas Church in Leipzig.

   _____

3. . . . moved from Bonn to Vienna.

   _____

4. . . . became deaf.

   _____

5. . . . became blind.

   _____

D Complete the analogies.

1. Ludwig: van Beethoven   = _____: Bach

2. *St. Matthew Passion*: _____ = *Eine Kleine Nachtmusik*: Mozart

3. _____: Beethoven = *Die Zauberflöte*: Mozart

4. Bach: Eisenach   = Mozart: _____

5. harpsichord and organ works: Bach   = 41 symphonies: _____

E Match the composer with his style of music.

1. _____ Bach   A. Classical

2. _____ Beethoven   B. Baroque

3. _____ Mozart   C. Romantic

F Match the illustrations with the names.

Bach
Mozart
Beethoven

1. _____

Die Musik

2. _____

3. _____

G **Can you name. . .?**

1. a rock group

    _____

2. a popular contemporary male singer

    _____

3. a popular contemporary female singer

    _____

H **Du bist dran! Choose one of following composers, and find out as much as you can about the person's life and musical works. Report to the class about your findings. A musical excerpt from an audiocassette or CD would add a nice touch to your presentation. Here is a list of possible composers: Josef Haydn, Clara Schumann, Robert Schumann, Johannes Brahms, Franz Schubert, Richard Wagner, Felix Mendelssohn, Anton Bruckner, and Arnold Schönberg. You may also want to research one of the new bands introduced in this unit.**

Lebendige Sprache

A

20.00 Nürnberg
Meistersingerhalle: 5. Philharmonisches Konzert, Werke von Béla Bartók und L. v. Beethoven, 19.15 Uhr Konzerteinführung
Sebalduskirche: The King's Consort, Eröffnungskonzert 55. ION Musica Sacra 2006
Tafelhalle: »speak«, Rodolpho Leoni Dance

B

ORGELMITTAGSKONZERT I

Montag
22. Mai
12.15 Uhr

Frauenkirche

Preis:
9,00 €

Johann Pachelbel
Toccata e-Moll
Johann Sebastian Bach
Passacaglia und Fuge c-Moll BWV 582
Choralpartita »Ach was soll ich Sünder« BWV 770
Max Reger
Ave Maria op. 80 Nr. 5
Camille Saint-Saëns
Deuxième Fantaisie op. 101

Johannes Unger, Orgel

Der renommierte junge Organist der Leipziger Thomaskirche und Preisträger zahlreicher internationaler Wettbewerbe präsentiert deutsche und französische Orgelwerke des Barock und der Romantik, darunter Saint-Saëns' großartige Fantaisie und Bachs berühmte Passacaglia und Fuge c-Moll.

D

20.00 Nürnberg
Gostner Hoftheater im Loft:
Grooveyard, Konzert
Sebalduskirche: Abschlusskonzert 55. ION, Bach Collegium
Sebalduskirche: Johann Sebastian Bach Orchestersuite Nr. 1 C-Dur BWV 1066 u. a.
Tafelhalle: „It is written", Peter Apfelbaum & The New York Hieroglyphics

C

Die Hochzeit des Figaro.
Oper von W. A. Mozart;
Komische Oper;. 18.45 Uhr.

E

Die Zauberflöte. Oper von W. A. Mozart; Deutsche Oper

F

19.00 Nürnberg
St. Peterskirche, Regensburger Str. 62:
Geistliches Konzert, Bach, Mendelssohn, Leinberger

G

19.30 Fürth
Stadttheater: „Die Entführung aus dem Serail", Singspiel von J. G. Stephanie, Musik W. A. Mozart

H

ORGELMITTAGSKONZERT II

Francis Pott
Toccata
William Byrd
»A Fancy for my Lady Nevelle«
Johann Pachelbel
Aria Tertia (Hexachordum Apollonis, 1699)
Johann Sebastian Bach
Praeludium und Fuge e-Moll BWV 548
Choralvorspiel »Dies sind die heilgen zehn Gebot« BWV 679
Charles Villiers Stanford
Fantasia und Toccata

Robert Quinney, Orgel

Dienstag
23. Mai
12.15 Uhr

Frauenkirche

Preis:
9,00 €

Der brillante junge britische Organist Robert Quinney, zweiter Organist der Westminster Abbey, präsentiert einzigartige englische Kompositionen aus drei Jahrhunderten zusammen mit einem großen Bachschen Meisterwerk.

Beethoven-Haus

Bonngasse 20
53111 Bonn
Tel. 02 28 / 98 175-25
Fax 02 28 / 98 175-26
E-mail: info@beethoven-haus-bonn.de

Öffnungszeiten:
1. April bis 31. Oktober Mo - Sa 10 - 18 Uhr,
Sonn- und Feiertage 11 - 18 Uhr
1. November bis 31. März Mo -Sa 10 - 17 Uhr,
Sonn- und Feiertage 11 - 17 Uhr
Eintritt: Erwachsene 4,– €,
Schüler/Studenten/Gruppen p.P. 3,– €

I You have become somewhat familiar with the three great musicians Bach, Mozart, and Beethoven. The ads below reflect some performances involving their masterpieces. Match each description with its respective performance labeled A–H.

_____ 1. Mozart's opera "The Magic Flute" is performed in the *Deutsche Oper*.

_____ 2. Bach's musical selection is played on an organ on May 22nd.

_____ 3. Mozart's music is heard in the City Theater of Fürth.

_____ 4. Ludwig van Beethoven's music is performed in the *Meistersingerhalle*.

_____ 5. The young British organist Robert Quinney plays organ music by Bach.

_____ 6. This Bach concert is performed at 8 p.m. in Nürnberg.

_____ 7. This concert is in the *St. Peterskirche* and includes two musicians in addition to Bach.

_____ 8. Mozart's "Marriage of Figaro" begins at 6:45 p.m.

J As you have read, Beethoven was born in Bonn. Look at the information provided and answer these questions.

1. What is the cost for students to visit Beethoven's home where he was born? _____

2. What is the zip code of Bonn? _____

3. On which day during the winter is this house opened the fewest hours? _____

4. How can you contact the information office of the *Beethoven-Haus* without sending a letter or calling by phone? _____

5. What do you think the word *Erwachsene* means? _____

6. How many hours on Mondays during the month of May are the exhibits open? _____

Sprichwort

Das ist Musik in meinen Ohren.
That's music to my ears.

Symtalk

K Ergänze die richtigen Wörter auf Deutsch! *(In the space, write the correct word in German.)*

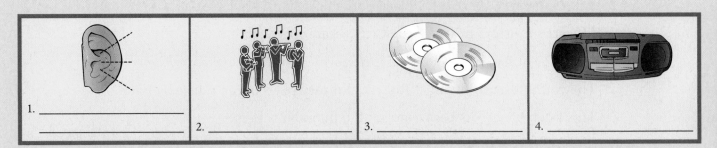

1. _____
   _____

2. _____

3. _____

4. _____

L Sag die Sätze! Dann schreib sie auf Deutsch! *(Say the sentences, then write them in German.)*

1.

_____

2.

_____

3.

_____

4.

_____

5.   _____

M **Mit einem Klassenkameraden, stell die Frage oder gib die Antwort!** (*With a classmate, ask the question or give the answer. Then, write the dialogue.*)

1.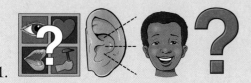

_____   _____

2.

_____   _____

3.

_____   _____

4.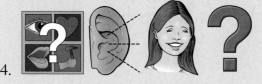

_____   _____

Kreuzworträtsel

Waagerecht

1. Bach's kind of music
5. Mozart's kind of music
6. legendary superstar
8. Bach's *Brandenburg* _____
10. birthplace of Beethoven
11. a Mozart symphony
12. *Die Zauberflöte* is example of an _____.

Senkrecht

2. Thomas _____ is a bass/baritone singer.
3. birthplace of Bach
4. famous older band
7. birthplace of Mozart
9. Mey, Grönemeyer, Nena, and Stürmer are all _____.
10. *Fettes* _____ is a hip-hop band.

UNIT 15

Das Wetter und die Jahreszeiten
Weather and Seasons

Vokabeln

Wie ist das Wetter? How's the weather?

Es ist schön. It's beautiful.

Es ist heiß. It's hot.

Es ist sonnig. **Es ist warm.**
It's sunny. It's warm.

Es ist kühl. **Es ist windig.** **Es ist schwül.** **Es ist wolkig.**
It's cool. It's windy. It's humid. It's cloudy.

Es ist schlecht. It is bad.

Es donnert. **Es regnet.** **Es blitzt.** **Es ist kalt.** **Es schneit.**
It's thundering. It's raining. There's lightning. It's cold. It's snowing.

Welche Jahreszeit haben wir?
What's the season?

Die vier Jahreszeiten

der Sommer

der Frühling

der Winter

der Herbst

- **im** Frühling/Sommer/Herbst/Winter = **in (the)** spring/summer/fall/winter
- Notice the noun forms of some verbs:

der Donner	=	thunder	→	**Es donnert.**	=	It's thundering.
der Blitz	=	lightning	→	**Es blitzt.**	=	It's lightning.
der Regen	=	rain	→	**Es regnet.**	=	It's raining.
der Schnee	=	snow	→	**Es schneit.**	=	It's snowing.
die Sonne	=	sun	→	**Die Sonne scheint.**	=	The sun is shining.

Mutter: *Trage* deinen Regenschirm!
Kind: Warum?
Mutter: Es regnet.

Mutter: Trage deine Sonnenbrille!
Kind: Warum?
Mutter: Es ist *sehr* sonnig.

Vater: Trage deinen Hut!
Kind: Warum?
Vater: Es ist *sehr* kalt.

| Trage | = | wear |
| sehr | = | very |

Übungen

A **Verbinde jede Abbildung mit einem Satz!** *(Match each picture with a sentence.)*

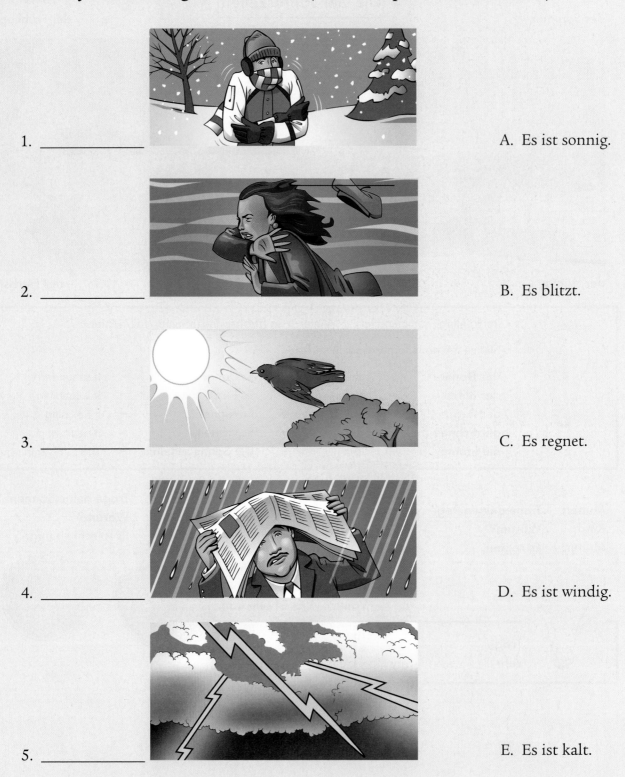

1. _____

A. Es ist sonnig.

2. _____

B. Es blitzt.

3. _____

C. Es regnet.

4. _____

D. Es ist windig.

5. _____

E. Es ist kalt.

Wie ist das Wetter? Beantworte diese Frage der Abbildung nach auf Deutsch! *(How's the weather? Answer this question in German according to each picture.)*

1. _____

2. _____

3. _____

4. _____

5. _____

C **Verbinde die Jahreszeit mit der Abbildung!** *(Match the picture with the season.)*

1. _____

A. der Sommer

2. _____

B. der Winter

3. _____

C. der Frühling

4. _____

D. der Herbst

D Write in *Column 1* the English meaning of each German word. When you have finished the entire column, cover the column of German words at the left. Then in *Column 2*, change the English words into German.

	Column 1 *English*	Column 2 *German*
1. Sonne	_____	_____
2. Blitz	_____	_____
3. Frühling	_____	_____
4. Sommer	_____	_____
5. Wetter	_____	_____
6. Herbst	_____	_____
7. Jahreszeit	_____	_____
8. kühl	_____	_____
9. heiß	_____	_____
10. Es regnet.	_____	_____
11. Winter	_____	_____
12. schlecht	_____	_____
13. Donner	_____	_____
14. kalt	_____	_____

E Match column *A* with column *B*.

A		B
1. _____	der Regen	A. scheinen
2. _____	der Schnee	B. donnern
3. _____	der Donner	C. blitzen
4. _____	der Blitz	D. schneien
5. _____	die Sonne	E. regnen

F *Wie ist das Wetter?* **Using the cues, write statements in German about the weather.**

1. mittens and parka

   _____

2. sunglasses

   _____

3. lightning rod

   _____

4. light sweater

   _____

5. outdoor tennis court

   _____

6. umbrella

   _____

7. snowflakes

   _____

8. air conditioner

   _____

9. sailboat

   _____

10. rain, wind, and hail

   _____

G **Lies den Absatz und dann wähle die richtigen Antworten!** *(Read the passage, and then complete the following sentences.)*

> Im Winter ist es sehr kalt. Es schneit viel. Der Schnee ist weiß. Im Frühling ist es windig und kühl und es regnet viel. Das Wetter im Sommer ist sonnig und heiß. Im Herbst ist es kühl und windig. Die vier Jahreszeiten sind sehr interessant.

1. **Wie ist das Wetter im Winter?**
   A. Es ist schwül.
   B. Es ist heiß.
   C. Es ist kalt.
   D. Es ist warm.

2. **Es regnet viel im ____.**
   A. Frühling
   B. Sommer
   C. Winter
   D. Herbst

3. **Es ist sehr heiß im ____.**
   A. Winter
   B. Herbst
   C. Frühling
   D. Sommer

4. **Es gibt ____ Jahreszeiten.**
   A. fünf
   B. vier
   C. sechs
   D. drei

H **Zum Sprechen. Think of three clothing items or accessories. For each one you select, ask your speaking partner to say how the weather is. Then reverse the roles. He/she will suggest to you three new cues and you should answer.**

> Beispiel: A: *die Sonnenbrille*
> *Wie ist das Wetter?*
> B: *Es ist sonnig.*

I **Du bist dran! Select five cities in various parts of the world and five different months. Use cities in different continents and hemispheres. Ask your partner about the weather in that city. Your partner then should respond appropriately according to the city and month. Don't forget that when it's summer in the northern hemisphere, it is winter in the southern hemisphere! Write your answers on a piece of paper.**

> Beispiel: A: *Wie ist das Wetter in Tokio (Tokyo) im January?*
> B: *Es ist kalt.*

Sprichwort

Morgenstund' hat Gold im Mund.

Early to bed and early to rise makes a man healthy, wealthy, and wise.

Lebendige Sprache

Das Wetter am Mittwoch, 26. April

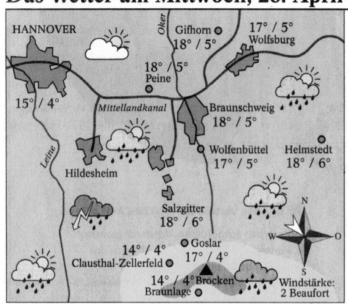

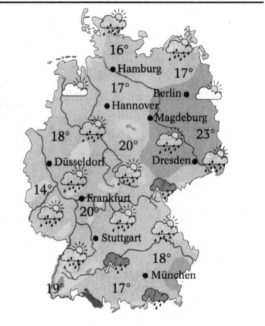

Zwischen Harz und Heide

Nur hier und da kommt mal die Sonne hervor. Meist überwiegen Wolken. Zeitweise fallen teilweise kräftige Schauer, örtlich begleitet von Blitz und Donner. Die Höchsttemperaturen erreichen 14 bis 18 Grad. In den höheren Lagen des Harzes verharren die Werte zwischen 6 und 10 Grad. Nachts kühlt sich die Luft in den tieferen Lagen auf 6 bis 4 Grad ab.

	14°	13°	12°	15°
	3°	3°	4°	5°
	DO	FR	SA	SO

Wetter für 12 Uhr Ortszeit

Berlin	Gewitter	21°	Köln/Bonn	Regenschauer	18°
Bremen	Regenschauer	17°	München	Gewitter	17°
Brocken	Regen	6°	Norderney	wolkig	13°
Dresden	Gewitter	23°	Sylt	wolkig	11°
Freiburg	Regenschauer	19°	Athen	sonnig	23°
Garmisch	Gewitter	15°	Barcelona	wolkig	24°
Bozen	Regenschauer	22°	Paris	wolkig	18°
Innsbruck	Gewitter	20°	Prag	sonnig	22°
London	sonnig	19°	Rom	Regen	18°
Mallorca	sonnig	22°	Teneriffa	heiter	23°
Moskau	wolkig	12°	Warschau	wolkig	22°
Nizza	Regenschauer	21°	Zürich	Regenschauer	17°

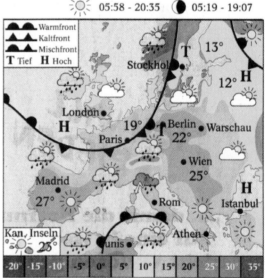

☀ 05:58 - 20:35   🌙 05:19 - 19:07

Europa

Vom Atlantik kommt feuchte und allmählich wieder kühlere Luft nach Mitteleuropa. Eher herbstlich als frühlingshaft ist es noch in Schottland. In England klettert das Quecksilber dagegen bis 19 Grad. Noch wärmere Temperaturen findet man rund um das Mittelmeer.

J *Wie ist das Wetter in. . .?* **Look at the regional map (upper left) and the Germany map (upper right) and answer this question.**

> **Beispiel:** A: *Wie ist das Wetter in Dresden?*
> B: *Es regnet und die Sonne scheint.*

1. München: _____

2. Magdeburg: _____

3. Hannover: _____

4. Stuttgart: _____

5. Der Brocken *(mountain in the south):*_____

6. Düsseldorf: _____

K *Wie warm ist es in. . .?* **The temperatures indicated are in centigrade. Write out (in German) the temperatures for the cities listed. In the regional map there are two temperatures given, the first is the daytime temperature and the second one is the nighttime temperature.**

> **Beispiel:** *Salzgitter =* <u>*achtzehn und sechs Grad* (degrees)</u>

1. Wolfsburg = _____

2. Frankfurt = _____

3. Clausthal-Zellerfeld = _____

4. Helmstedt = _____

5. Hamburg = _____

6. Peine = _____

L **Write the name of the capital cities *(auf Deutsch)* for the following countries.**

1. England: _____

2. Germany: _____

3. Italy: _____

4. France: _____

5. Spain: _____

6. Poland: _____

7. Sweden: _____

8. Greece: _____

Symtalk

M   **Ergänze die richtigen Wörter auf Deutsch!** *(In the space, write the correct word in German.)*

1. _____   2. _____   3. _____   4. _____   5. _____

N   **Sag die Sätze! Dann schreib sie auf Deutsch!** *(Say the sentences, then write them in German.)*

1. _____

2. _____

3. _____

4. _____

5. _____

O **Mit einem Klassenkameraden, stell die Frage oder gib die Antwort!** *(With a classmate, ask the question or give the answer. Then, write the dialogue.)*

1.

_____ Nein, _____

2.

_____ Nein, _____

3.

_____ Ja, _____

4.

_____ Nein, _____

5.

_____ Nein, _____

Kreuzworträtsel

Note: ß = SS

Waagerecht

1. season of new flowers
5. kite flying weather: *Es ist* _____.
6. gives us warmth and light
7. weather in the winter
8. time for some animals to hibernate
10. season after *Frühling*
11. A temperate climate has four _____.
12. opposite of *schön*

Senkrecht

2. season after *Sommer*
3. big noise during a storm
4. weather in the summer
5. *Wie ist das* _____?
7. not so *kalt*
9. time for a *Regenschirm: Es* _____.
10. nice pleasant weather: *Es ist* _____.

Unit 16

Die Tage und die Monate
Days and Months

Vokabeln

Welcher Tag ist heute?　　**Heute ist . . .**

What day is today?　　Today is . . .

Monday **Montag**	**Dienstag**	**Mittwoch**	**Donnerstag**	**Freitag**	**Samstag** **(Sonnabend)**	**Sonntag**
	1	2	3	4	5	6
7	8	9	10	11	12	13
14	15	16	17	18	19	20
21	22	23	24	25	26	27
28	29	30	31			

Wann ist der Feiertag?	When is the holiday?
Er ist morgen.	It's tomorrow.
Welches Datum haben wir heute?	What is the date today?
Heute ist der erste August.	It's August first.
der dritte Oktober	October 3rd (Day of German Unity)
29.5. (29. Mai)	5/29 (May 29)

März
April
Mai

September
Oktober
November

Juni
Juli
August

Dezember
Januar
Februar

- **Ordinal Numbers**
  the first *der erste*; the second *der zweite*; the third *der dritte*
  the fourth to the nineteenth: add *te* to the number (*der vierte, der neunzehnte*)
  the twentieth to the thirty-first: add *ste* (*der zwanzigste*)

- **Dates**
  When writing the date, always put the day of the month before the month: *8.12.* =
  December 8. Example: Sunday, December 8th = *Sonntag, der achte Dezember/der*
  8. Dezember

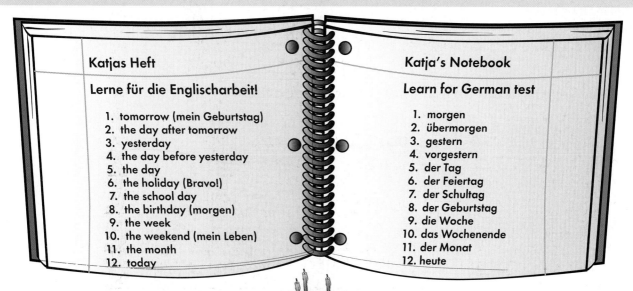

Katjas Heft

Lerne für die Englischarbeit!

1. tomorrow (mein Geburtstag)
2. the day after tomorrow
3. yesterday
4. the day before yesterday
5. the day
6. the holiday (Bravo!)
7. the school day
8. the birthday (morgen)
9. the week
10. the weekend (mein Leben)
11. the month
12. today

Katja's Notebook

Learn for German test

1. morgen
2. übermorgen
3. gestern
4. vorgestern
5. der Tag
6. der Feiertag
7. der Schultag
8. der Geburtstag
9. die Woche
10. das Wochenende
11. der Monat
12. heute

Tim: **Wann hast du Geburtstag, Jens?**
When is your birthday, Jens?

Jens: **Er ist übermorgen, am achten Juni.**
It's the day after tomorrow, on June eighth.

Maja: **An welchem Tag ist die Englischarbeit?**
What day is the English test?

Michael: **Sie ist am Dienstag.**
It's on Tuesday.

	Dienstag	Mittw...
	1	2
7	8	9
	15	

Laura: **Was hast du heute, Andreas?**
What do you have today, Andreas?

Andreas: **Ich habe gar nichts.**
Heute habe ich frei.
Nothing! Today I've got a free day.

Bettina: **Was hast du am Mittwoch?**
What do you have on Wednesday?

Natascha: **Ich habe meine Klavierstunde.**
I have my piano lesson.

Weekdays and Mythology

Derivations and Comparisons

German Day	Norse Mythology
Montag	Day honoring the moon god (*Mond* = moon).
Dienstag	Day honoring Tyr, a god of war, and Mars Thingsus, the Roman god of war. *Dienstag* was tribal meeting day.
Mittwoch	Day honoring Odin or Wodan, father of all the gods and a god of war. Wodan's day = Wednesday. Wodan often wore a hat with a wide brim and carried a large staff. The Romans compared him to Mercury, who also had a large staff (caduseus). (The early Christians abolished "Wodan's Day" and substituted "Mid-week.")
Donnerstag	Day honoring Thor, god of weather and son of Wodan. Thor = *Donner* = thunder. Thor's Day = Thursday. Thor always carried a big hammer. The Romans thought he was like their own Hercules, who also carried a club.
Freitag	Day honoring Freya, or Freia, the goddess of love and wife of Wodan. The Romans found her similar to their goddess Venus.
Samstag	Day related to seeds, planting, and the Roman god Saturn
Sonntag	Day honoring the sun god; *die Sonne* = sun

Übungen

A Write in numerical form the dates that your teacher reads.

> **Beispiel:** Teacher says: der dreißigste Dezember
> You write: 30.12.

1. _____

2. _____

3. _____

4. _____

5. _____

B Label the current month. Include the names of the days and all the numbers.

C **Schreib die Daten!** *(Write the dates.)*

> **Beispiel:** Tuesday, February 11th
> Dienstag, der 11. Februar

1. Wednesday, October 22

   _____

2. Sunday, August 13th

   _____

3. Thursday, May 1st

   _____

4. Friday, April 26th

   _____

5. Saturday, February 9th

   _____

D **Answer the following in English.**

1. If the German date is 5.3., what is the month and what is the day?

   _____

2. What do you hear when Thor, the weather god, strikes his hammer?

   _____

3. Identify by names the family of gods represented in the weekdays.

   mother: _____

   father: _____

   son: _____

E **Wähle die richtigen Antworten!** *(Choose the correct answers.)*

1. Welcher Tag ist morgen?
   A. Woche
   B. Montag
   C. Juli
   D. Monat

2. Welches Datum haben wir heute?
   A. Heute ist ein Feiertag.
   B. Heute habe ich frei.
   C. Heute ist der zweite Februar.
   D. Heute ist Sonntag.

The following questions are based on the dialogues presented in this unit. Review them before you choose your answers.

3. Was hat Jens am 8. Juni?
   A. ein Wochenende
   B. März
   C. Geburtstag
   D. Freitag

4. Was hast du am Dienstag, Michael?
   A. Ich habe eine Englischarbeit.
   B. Ich habe einen Hund und zwei Katzen.
   C. Ich habe ein Haus in Köln.
   D. Ich habe eine kleine Familie.

5. An welchem Tag ist Nataschas Klavierstunde?
   A. am Montag
   B. am Mittwoch
   C. am Sonntag
   D. am Dienstag

6. Wer hat heute frei?
   A. Andreas
   B. Jen
   C. Bettina
   D. Laura

F   **Verbinde das Deutsch mit dem Englisch.** *(Match the German with the English.)*

1. _____ heute
2. _____ übermorgen
3. _____ vorgestern
4. _____ morgen
5. _____ gestern

A. day after tomorrow
B. yesterday
C. today
D. tomorrow
E. day before yesterday

G   **Schreib auf Deutsch!** *(Write in German.)*

1. the third month of the year

   _____

2. the day that honors the Norse god, Thor

   _____

3. the day that honors the Norse goddess, Freya

   _____

4. the month that brings May flowers

   _____

5. the first day of the German week

   _____

6. the month of the German Unity Day

   _____

7. the month in which Valentine's Day is celebrated

   _____

8. the month of your *Geburtstag*

   _____

Schreib den deutschen Tag der Abbildung nach! *(Identify the German weekday according to the illustration.)*

1. _____

2. _____

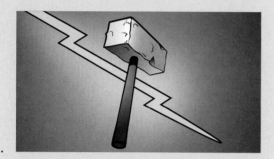

3. _____

4. _____

5. _____

6. _____

7. _____

I **Lies den Absatz und dann wähle die richtigen Antworten!** *(Read the paragraph and then select the correct answers.)*

> Heute ist ein sehr guter Tag für Dieter, einen österreichischen Jungen aus Salzburg. Er *besucht* seinen Freund Ebi in München. Es ist Samstag, der 9. Juli. Es ist auch der *letzte* Tag der *Fußballweltmeisterschaft*. Deutschland *spielt gegen* Italien für den *Weltpokal*. *Die beiden Mannschaften* spielen in München. Dieter und Ebi haben Glück. Sie gehen *bald* in das Stadion. Dieter ist sehr glücklich.

besucht	is visiting	**Weltpokal**	World Cup
letzte	last	**die beiden Mannschaften**	both teams
Fußballweltmeisterschaft	soccer world cup	**bald**	soon
spielt gegen	is playing against		

1. Welcher Tag ist heute?
   - A. Samstag
   - B. Freitag
   - C. Dienstag
   - D. Sonntag

2. Was ist das Datum?
   - A. der zehnte Juli
   - B. der neunte Juli
   - C. der zwölfte Juli
   - D. der elfte Juli

3. Wer ist Ebi?
   - A. der Bruder von Dieter
   - B. der Onkel von Dieter
   - C. der Lehrer von Dieter
   - D. der Freund von Dieter

4. Wo ist das Fußballspiel?
   - A. in Österreich
   - B. in Italien
   - C. in Deutschland
   - D. in England

5. Wie ist Dieter?
   - A. glücklich
   - B. traurig
   - C. krank
   - D. interessant

J   **Zum Sprechen.** **Find out from your speaking partner on what day three things are: his/her birthday *(der Geburtstag)*, his/her music lesson *(die Musikstunde)* and his/her test *(die Arbeit)*. Start with *An welchem Tag ist. . .?* He/she should answer by saying a specific day of the week. Then he/she will ask you when three other things are: *der Feiertag, der Geburtstag von . . .* and *das Picknick,* and he/she should start with *Wann ist. . .?* You should answer with a general time such as today, tomorrow, or the day after tomorrow.**

K   **Du bist dran!** **Find out whether you and your classmate know your days of the week. You start by saying, *"Heute ist Montag."* Your classmate says, *"Morgen ist Dienstag."* You finish by saying *"Übermorgen ist Mittwoch."* Then your partner goes back to: *"Heute ist. . .,"* etc. Continue until you both have identified all of the weekdays.**

nationaltheater mannheim

SPIELPLAN 4.11. bis 12.11.

OPERNHAUS

SA. 04.11.	20.00	**DIE SCHÖPFUNG** Abo B, ThG blau*/Preise B
SO. 05.11.	Ab 10.00	**BRUNCH IM FOYER**
	'11.00	**JAZZFRÜHSCHOPPEN**
	16.00-21.40	**GÖTTERDÄMMERUNG** (Wiederaufnahme) Abo NA*/ Preise A
	Anschließend	**NACHGEHAKT** (Oberes Foyer)
Mi. 08.11.	11.00-13.00	**PAPAGENO SPIELT AUF DER ZAUBERFLÖTE***
DO. 09.11.	20.00-22.45	**EIN MASKENBALL** ThG 5831-6360, 6891-7420, ThG rot*/Preise C, Unikat ab PG III
FR. 10.11.	19.30-22.45	**DIE ZAUBERFLÖTE** (Wiederaufnahme) ThG 4771-5300, 7951-8480*/Preise B, Unikat ab PG III
SA. 11.11.	15.00-17.00	**CAFÉ CONCERT** (Oberes Foyer)
	20.00-22.45	**TURANDOT***/Preise B
SO. 12.11.	Ab 10.00	**BRUNCH IM FOYER**
	11.00	**KAMMERMUSIKALISCHE MATINÉE: WALZER IM QUADRAT** (Schauspielhaus)*/
	18.30	**KURZEINFÜHRUNG** (Oberes Foyer)
	19.00	**COMBATTIMENTO DI TANCREDI E CLORINDA/HERZOG BLAUBARTS BURG** Abo G*/Preise B
	Anschließend	**NACHGEHAKT** (Oberes Foyer)

SCHAUSPIELHAUS

SA. 04.11.	19.30	**DIE VERSCHWÖRUNG DES FIESCO ZU GENUA***/Preise E
SO. 05.11.	20.00	**DAS BLUT** (DE) Abo W2*/Preise E
MO. 06.11.	19.00	**KURZEINFÜHRUNG** (Foyer)
	19.30	**DIE VERSCHWÖRUNG DES FIESCO ZU GENUA***/Preise F
DI. 07.11.	18.00	Geschlossene Veranstaltung der Deutschen Bank
FR. 10.11.	20.00	**LEONCE UND LENA** ThG 6361-6890*/Preise E
SA. 11.11.	20.00	**SEKAI** (Premiere)*/Preise C
SO. 12.11.	20.00	**SEKAI***/Preise E

WERKHAUS

MI. 08.11.	19.30	**KURZEINFÜHRUNG** (Studio)
	20.00	**PHAIDRAS LIEBE** (Studio)*
	Anschließend	**NACHGEHAKT** (Studio)
FR. 10.11.	20.00	**APROPOS „FIESCO"** hypersound concrète (Studio)*
SO. 12.11.	20.00	**PHAIDRAS LIEBE** (Studio)*

SCHNAWWL

DI. 07.11.	19.00	**PÄDAGOGEN-JOUR-FIXE**
MI. 08.11.	19.00-21.10	Öffenliche Hauptprobe für Pädagoginnen: **DER METEORITENLÖFFEL** Bitte anmelden!
SA. 11.11.	19.00-21.10	**DER METEORITENLÖFFEL** (Premiere)*

*= Freier Verkauf - Änderungen vorbehalten!
Kartentelefon: Di. bis Fr. 9.00-17.00 Uhr, Mo. und Sa. 9.00-13.00 Uhr

Nationaltheater • Tel. (06 21) 16 80-150; Fax (06 21) 16 80 - 258
Schnawwl • Tel. (06 21) 16 80 - 302

101549489_6917270

L Look at the schedule from the *Nationaltheater Mannheim*. Indicate the day of the week on which each performance takes place. *Auf Deutsch, bitte!*

> **Beispiel** *Kurzeinführung* (Studio): <u>*Am Mittwoch.*</u>

1. Brunch im Foyer: _____

2. Die Verschwörung des Fiesco zu Genua: _____

3. Die Schöpfung: _____

4. Der Meteoritenlöffel (Premiere): _____

5. Die Zauberflöte: _____

6. Papageno spielt auf der Zauberflöte: _____

7. Ein Maskenball: _____

8. Geschlossene Veranstaltung der Deutschen Bank: _____

M Answer the following questions in English.

1. In which month do these performances take place?

_____

2. At what time do most of the performances begin?

_____

3. On which days can you order tickets by phone until 5 p.m.?

_____

4. Which performance is the longest? How long is it?

_____

Sprichwort

Morgen, morgen, nur nicht heute, sagen alle faulen Leute.
Don't put off until tomorrow what you can do today.

Symtalk

N
Ergänze die richtigen Wörter auf Deutsch! *(In the space, write the corret word in German.)*

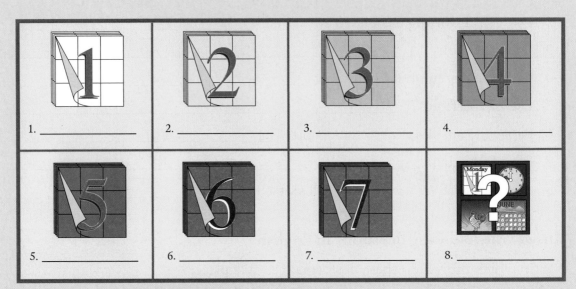

1. _____

2. _____

3. _____

4. _____

5. _____

6. _____

7. _____

8. _____

O **Lies die Sätze! Dann schreib sie auf Deutsch!** *(Read the sentences, then write them in German.)*

1.

_____

2.

_____

3.

_____

4.

_____

Mit einem Klassenkameraden, stell die Frage oder gib die Antwort! *(With a classmate, ask the question or give the answer. Then, write the dialogue.)*

1.

_____

2.

_____

3.

_____

4.

_____

5.

_____

Kreuzworträtsel

Waagerecht

1. from Friday afternoon until Sunday evening
5. month of the year's first holiday
6. a weekend day
8. month of Martians
9. date
10. day honoring the god of heat and light
11. a summer month
12. One attends classes on a ____.
14. Today is the tomorrow worried about ____.

Senkrecht

2. *gestern, ____ und morgen*
3. day when Thor might throw his hammer
4. opposite of *Abend*
7. day in the middle of the week
8. day honoring the god of the moon
13. *Guten ___*

UNIT 17

Die Literatur

Literature

Berühmte Autoren

Johann Wolfgang von Goethe

1749–1832

Johann Wolfgang von Goethe (1749–1832), considered by many to be Germany's greatest writer, was born in Frankfurt. He studied at several universities, excelling at law, art, science, politics, and literature. He held several positions: statesman; theater director; newspaper editor; and internationally famous poet, dramatist, and novelist. Goethe's work enabled him to travel widely, and his command of languages permitted him to be at home almost anywhere. He did research in many areas of science and even illustrated his scientific studies.

In his Classical drama *Faust* the author wrote about a situation common to most human beings: the desire for fame or pleasure as opposed to spiritual values. The scientist Faust promises the devil that he will give up his religious faith if, in exchange, all his desires for knowledge and power can be satisfied. The drama *Faust* inspired the composers Gounod and Berlioz to write operas presenting this conflict. Goethe's other Classical works include the drama *Iphigenie auf Tauris* and a two-part novel called *Wilhelm Meister*. His poems cover several styles and many themes. A romantic novel called *Die Leiden des jungen Werthers (The Sorrows of Young Werther)* became an immediate bestseller in Europe.

Friedrich Schiller (1759–1805) was born in the little city of Marbach in southwestern Germany. Although he studied law and medicine at the university, he much preferred literature. He became a writer at the Mannheim Theater, a professor of history at Jena, and a friend of Goethe's at Weimar.

Schiller wrote many plays that revolve around classical ideals, such as freedom, duty, and love. His characters deal with major problems and have to make important decisions. In *Maria Stuart,* the Scottish queen Mary Stuart, accepts her unjust imprisonment by Elisabeth as atonement for her own misdeeds. In the patriotic play *Wilhelm Tell,* the hero William chooses between the possible death of his son and the freedom of the Swiss people. In the poem *"An die Freude"* (Ode to Joy), Schiller shares his belief that love can make the world a better place. Beethoven incorporated this poem into his Ninth Symphony. (This work was played when the Berlin Wall came down in 1989. An instrumental version is now the official anthem of the European Union.)

Friedrich Schiller

1759–1805

Ernst Theodor Amadeus Hoffmann (1776–1822) was born in Königsberg on the Baltic Sea. He was a musician as well as a writer. He loved the music of Mozart so much that he changed his second middle name from Wilhelm to Amadeus.

Hoffmann's writing influenced authors in other nations, especially Charles Baudelaire in France and Edgar Allen Poe in the United States. A collection of his stories *Nachtstücke* inspired Offenbach's opera *Les Contes d'Hoffmann* or *The Tales of Hoffmann*. The story *Nussknacker und Mausekönig* inspired Tschaikovsky's musical work *The Nutcracker Suite*. Hoffmann's stories are Romantic. They deal with imagination and with the many opposites in everyday life: joy and sorrow, good and evil, dreams and reality, and night and day.

E.T.A. Hoffmann

1776–1822

Else Lasker-Schüler (1869–1945) grew up at a time when it was difficult for a woman to get a good education. However, changes in the late nineteenth and early twentieth centuries provided increased opportunities for women. Lasker-Schüler joined the exciting circle of Berlin's Expressionists. She contributed to literary magazines and wrote several volumes of poetry. Artistically talented as well, the author decorated her books with her own drawings. Her works were praised by such celebrities as poet Gottfried Benn and artist Franz Marc.

Else Lasker-Schüler

1869–1945

Most of the author's poems, which are in volumes entitled *Styx, Der siebente Tag (The Seventh Day),* and *Hebräische Balladen (Hebrew Ballads)* are about the themes of love, friendship, and loss. They show the poet's unusual use of language and contain colorful imagery and references to mythology. In general they reflect the free spirit of the Expressionist movement. Gottfried Benn called Lasker-Schüler the greatest woman lyric poet of Germany!

Christa Wolf is a contemporary novelist. Born in 1929 in Landsberg (a German town then, now in Poland), she had to move with her family to eastern Germany after World War II. Wolf's first novel *Der geteilte Himmel (Divided Heaven)* received world wide attention and appeared as a motion picture.

Christa Wolf

Sarah Kirsch

It concerns two young people whose lives and love are disrupted by the politics of East versus West. A second novel, *Nachdenken über Christa T (Quest for Crista T.),* shows the conflict between a society's values and an individual's creativity. In the story *Kassandra* the author warns that if people forget to be loving and respectful of one another, they may end up destroying their culture and their humanity.

Sarah Kirsch, born in 1935, is a lyrical poet. Her original name was Ingrid but she changed it to Sarah, in honor of those victimized by the Nazis. As a writer in the German Democratic Republic, Kirsch wrote about the lives of working women *(Die Pantherfrau–The Panther Woman)* and translated works from Russian into German. She wrote many poems. In *Landaufenthalt (A Story in the Country),* she talks about nature and simple everyday things. She uses beautiful language to describe the beauty of flowers and birds. Her book *Zaubersprüche (Magic Spells)* has to do with the themes of love, relationships, persecution, and loss.

Famous German stories for children include:

1. **Heidi,** the story of the little mountain girl, by Swiss writer Johanna Spyri, 1881; motion picture version starred Shirley Temple

2. **Bambi,** the story of a forest deer, by Austrian writer Felix Salten, 1923; animated motion picture by Walt Disney

3. **Emil und die Detektive** *(Emil and the Detectives),* the story about how a boy and his friends capture a pickpocket, by German writer Erich Kästner, 1929

4. **Das doppelte Lottchen** *(Lottie and Lisa),* the story of twins who bring their feuding parents together again, by Erich Kästner, 1949; several film versions: in London called *Twice Upon a Time,* four Disney film versions called *The Parent Trap,* and two German versions called *Das doppelte Lottchen* and *Charlie und Louise.*

Erich Kästner

Die Literatur

Übungen

A Guess who...

1. . . . loved the music of Mozart and Beethoven. _____
2. . . . studied medicine. _____
3. . . . wrote poems about nature._____
4. . . . decorated her poetry with her own art. _____
5. . . . studied botany and optics. _____
6. . . . wrote about politics and love. _____

B Verbinde die Namen mit den Beschreibungen. *(Match the names with the descriptions.)*

1. _____ Else Lasker-Schüler
2. _____ "Romantic" stories
3. _____ Sarah
4. _____ "Classical" stories
5. _____ Ernst Theodor Amadeus

A. Kirsch
B. are about ideals
C. Expressionist poet
D. Hoffmann
E. are about dreams and imagination

C Following the example, complete the chart below.

Name of Work	Author	Type of Musical Version	Composer(s)
Beispiel: *Wilhelm Tell*	Schiller	opera	Rossini
1. *Nachtstücke*	_____	_____	_____
2. *An die Freude*	_____	_____	_____
3. *Nussknacker und Mausekönig*	_____	_____	_____
4. *Faust*	_____	_____	_____

D **Verbinde die Abbildung mit jedem Namen!** *(Match the picture with the name of the author.)*

1. _____

A. Goethe

2. _____

B. Hoffmann

3. _____

C. Schiller

E **Label each scenario described below as either Classical or Romantic.**

Eunice Unity is working this summer at Camp Ideal. Her job is to organize the children into activity groups and to direct a variety show for the benefit of underprivileged children. Today the campers are arguing about who has the most talent and who will perform first. Eunice arrives on the scene and, in a short time, transforms the children from selfish creatures into helpful and compassionate young people.

1. _____

While riding your horse one late moonlit evening, you come to a fork in the road. A sign pointing to the left says: *This way to that way.* A sign pointing to the right says: *That way to this way.* Just as you are about to make your decision, a cloud passes in front of the moon, an owl shrieks, and a poem flies into your face.

2. _____

F **Which author would most likely. . .**

1. . . . encourage a child to learn and enjoy many subjects?

_____

2. . . . enjoy creating new words and puns?

_____

3. . . . agree to give a lecture on Swiss or Scottish history?

_____

4. . . . understand the problems of hardworking people?

_____

5. . . . sign a petition to stop wars and save human rights?

_____

6. . . . wear an "I Love Mozart and Beethoven" T-shirt?

_____

G **Du bist dran! Choose one of the novels or plays mentioned in this chapter. Ask the librarian for help in finding the book and/or information about the plot. Carefully look over what you have found, and then, in your own words, retell the story to your classmates. You may wish to draw pictures on the board which relate to the story and the names of the main characters.**

Sprichwort

Wer A sagt, muss auch B sagen.
Finish what you start.

Lebendige Sprache

GOETHE-SCHILLER-DENKMAL
Seit 1857 stehen die beiden schon vor dem Weimarer Komödienhaus: fast auf gleicher Augenhöhe, aber ohne Blickkontakt—Goethe und Schiller vereint, in unterschiedliche Richtungen sehend, als Denkmal geschaffen von Ernst Rietschel. Kopien des Goethe-Schiller-Denkmals stehen in den US-amerikanischen Städten Cleveland, Milwaukee und San Francisco.

JOHANN-WOLFGANG VON GOETHE
Geheimrat, Dichter, Mediziner, Physiker-einfach Genius. Als junger Mann kam er 1775 auf Einladung des Herzogs Carl August nach Weimar—und blieb bis zu seinem Lebensende 1832.

FRIEDRICH SCHILLER
war Dichter, Dramatiker und Freund von Goethe. Ende Juli 1787 reiste Schiller nach seiner Flucht aus der Militärakademie einem neuen Teil seines Lebens entgegen. Er ging nach Weimar. 1802 erwarb er ein Haus an der Esplanade und wohnte hier mit seiner Familie bis zu seinem Tode 1805.

H As you read in this chapter, Goethe and Schiller are considered to be two of the most influential writers in German literature. Look at the articles and try to determine the answers.

Goethe-Schiller Denkmal

1. When was the statue built? _____

2. In which U.S. cities can you find replicas of this statue?

    _____

Johann Wolfgang von Goethe

3. When did Goethe come to Weimar? _____

4. When did Goethe die? _____

Friedrich Schiller

5. When did Schiller arrive in Weimar? _____

6. What kind of academy did Schiller attend? _____

Das doppelte Lottchen

7. Who wrote "Das doppelte Lottchen?" _____

8. Where is the theater located? _____

Spezialitäten aus aller Welt

9. From how many countries do the recipes in the cookbook come?

    _____

10. What do you think the German word for "world" is? _____

11. Write in German: I like to eat. _____

Im Land der Schokolade und Bananen

12. Who is the author of this book? _____

13. Can you guess what the title of the book in English is?

    _____

14. How many children come to a strange country? _____

Symtalk

I   **Ergänze die richtigen Wörter auf Deutsch!** *(In the space, write the correct word in German.)*

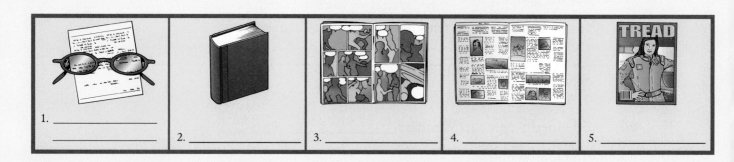

1. _____
_____

2. _____

3. _____

4. _____

5. _____

J   **Sag die Sätze! Dann schreib sie auf Deutsch!** *(Say the sentences, then write them in German.)*

1. _____

2. _____

3. _____

4. _____

_____

Beschreibe jede Szene! Auf Deutsch, bitte! *(In German, write a description of each scene.)*

1. _____
_____
_____
_____
_____

2. _____
_____
_____
_____
_____

3. _____
_____
_____
_____
_____

4. _____
_____
_____
_____
_____

Kreuzworträtsel

Waagerecht

1. author who wants people to care about each other
4. Goethe's city
7. what Kirsch likes to write about
10. poet who translated works from Russian into German
11. Schiller's city
12. Germany's greatest author

Senkrecht

2. scientist who made a deal with the devil
3. hero of a story by Hoffmann
5. Hoffmann's city
6. wrote historical plays
8. Kirsch's first name
9. Tell's first name

UNIT 18

Die Freizeit
Leisure and Recreation

Vokabeln

Wohin gehst du?
Where are you going?

Ich gehe zum Fußballspiel.
I'm going to the soccer game.

Ich gehe ins Museum.
I'm going to the museum.

Ich gehe auf die Party.
I'm going to the party.

Ich gehe zum Strand.
I'm going to the beach.

SOFIA:	**Wohin gehst du heute Abend?**	Where are you going tonight?
MICHAEL:	**Ich gehe zum Fußballspiel.**	I'm going to the soccer game.
SOFIA:	**Ich auch!**	I'm going, too!

❀❀❀❀❀

JOHANN:	**Was machst du heute?**	What are you doing today?
KATJA:	**Ich gehe ins Museum . . . in die Alte Pinakothek.***	I'm going to the museum . . . to the Alte Pinakothek.
JOHANN:	**Was ist da los?**	What's going on there?
KATJA:	**Das Dürerfest findet diese Woche statt.**	The Dürer Festival is taking place this week.

*The **Alte Pinakothek,** an art museum in München, houses paintings and works of art from the 14th to the 18th centuries. Its counterpart, the **Neue Pinakothek,** contains art generally from the 19th and 20th centuries.

Welche Sportart treibst du?
What sports do you play?

Ich spiele Fußball.
I play soccer.

Ich spiele Volleyball.
I play volleyball.

Ich spiele Tennis.
I play tennis.

Ich spiele Basketball.
I play basketball.

Ich spiele Baseball.
I play baseball.

Ich spiele amerikanischen Fußball. I play football.

Was machst du gern?
What do you like to do?

Ich laufe gern Ski.
I like to ski. / I like skiing.

Ich lese gern.
I like to read. / I like reading.

Ich tanze gern.
I like to dance. / I like dancing.

Ich reite gern.
I like horseback riding.

Ich schwimme gern.
I like to swim. / I like swimming.

Ich fahre gern Rad.
I like to ride my bike. / I like biking.

WILLI:	**Morgen machen wir ein Picknick.**	Tomorrow we're having a picnic.
ANTJE:	**Wo denn?**	Where?
WILLI:	**Am Strand. Willst du mitkommen?**	At the beach. Do you want to come along?
ANTJE:	**Ja. Ich schwimme gern.**	Yes. I like to swim.

❀❀❀❀❀

BETTINA:	**Gehst du heute Abend auch auf die Party?**	Are you going to the party tonight, too?
MARTIN:	**Na klar! Gibt es da Musik?**	Of course! Will there be music?
BETTINA:	**Ja, sicher! Ich tanze sehr gern.**	Yes, indeed. I love to dance.

Übungen

A **Wohin gehst du? Ergänze die Sätze auf Deutsch!** *(Where are you going? Complete the sentences in German, using the cues in parentheses.)*

1. Ich gehe zu einem _____. *(soccer game)*

2. Ich gehe zu einem _____. *(picnic)*

3. Ich gehe auf eine _____. *(party)*

4. Ich gehe in ein _____. *(museum)*

5. Ich gehe zum _____. *(beach)*

B **The following questions are based on all the dialogues presented in this unit. Review them before you choose the correct answers.**

1. Wann ist das Fußballspiel?
   A. am Montag
   B. um vier Uhr
   C. heute Abend
   D. in zwei Wochen

2. Was ist die Alte Pinakothek?
   A. ein Strand
   B. ein Museum
   C. ein Dürerfest
   D. ein Rad

3. Wer ist Dürer?
   A. ein Lehrer
   B. ein Onkel
   C. ein Museum
   D. ein Künstler

4. Wann ist das Picknick?
   A. morgen
   B. heute
   C. am Sonntag
   D. um ein Uhr

5. Wo ist das Picknick?
   A. am Mittwoch
   B. am Dienstag
   C. am Strand
   D. am Museum

C **Welche Sportart treibst du? Ergänze die Sätze auf Deutsch!** *(What sports do you play? Complete each sentence in German.)*

1. Ich spiele _____.

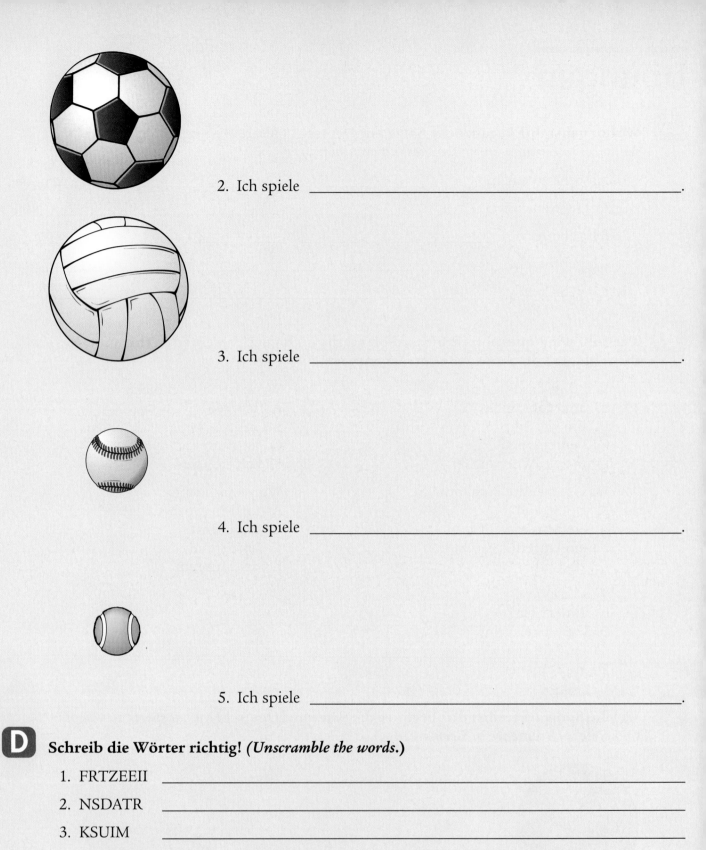

2. Ich spiele _____.

3. Ich spiele _____.

4. Ich spiele _____.

5. Ich spiele _____.

D **Schreib die Wörter richtig!** *(Unscramble the words.)*

1. FRTZEEII _____

2. NSDATR _____

3. KSUIM _____

4. KPCINKCI _____

5. EMMSUU _____

E **Was machst du gern? Ergänze die Sätze auf Deutsch!** *(What do you enjoy doing? Complete each sentence in German.)*

1. Ich _____ gern Ski.

2. Ich _____ gern.

3. Ich _____ gern ein Buch.

4. Ich _____ gern Rad.

5. Ich _____ gern.

6. Ich _____ gern.

7. Ich _____ gern.

F **Ergänze den Dialog auf Deutsch!** *(Complete the dialogue in German.)*

KARL LUDWIG: Was machst (1.) _____ am Freitag Abend?

BRIGITTE: (2.) _____ gehe zu Susannes Haus.

KARL LUDWIG: Was ist da (3.) _____?

BRIGITTE: Eine Party (4.) _____ da statt.

KARL LUDWIG: Wie viele gehen auf die (5.) _____?

BRIGITTE: Neun. Fünf (6.) _____ und vier Jungen.

KARL LUDWIG: Gut. Ich mache mit. Ich tanze (7.) _____.

G **Lies den Absatz! Wähle die richtigen Antworten!** *(Read the passage. Choose the appropriate answers.)*

Thomas hat heute eine Geburtstagsparty am Strand. Heute ist er vierzehn Jahre alt. Das Wetter ist warm und schön. Die Party beginnt um drei Uhr. Wer kommt zur Party? Sieben Freunde. Sie sind glücklich. Sie spielen Volleyball, schwimmen und tanzen. Es gibt viel zu essen und trinken: Butterbrote, Eis und *natürlich* einen *Geburtstagskuchen*. Ein Picknick am Strand ist eine *prima* Idee!

natürlich	naturally
Geburtstagskuchen	birthday cake
prima	terrific

1. Wie alt ist Thomas heute?
   A. 14
   B. 13
   C. 15
   D. 12

2. Wie ist das Wetter?
   A. kalt
   B. windig
   C. gut
   D. heiß

3. Wo ist die Party?
   A. am Strand
   B. im Museum
   C. im Restaurant
   D. auf dem Lande

4. Was spielen die Mädchen und Jungen?
   A. Tennis
   B. Fußball
   C. Baseball
   D. Volleyball

5. Wie sind Thomas und seine Freunde?
   A. krank
   B. glücklich
   C. traurig
   D. ungesund

H **Zum Sprechen!** Think of three places where you could go this weekend, i.e. a museum, a beach, a picnic. Your speaking partner will ask you where you are going and you should answer appropriately. Then reverse the roles, using new places.

> Beispiel: A: Wohin gehst du?
> B: Ich gehe zum Strand.

I **Du bist dran!** Try a word association game with a partner. Each of you will prepare a list of five nouns. You start by giving your partner your list. Within a set time frame, for example, one minute, he/she will say a word that in some way is related to each noun, for example: *ein Buch, lesen; ein Museum, die Alte Pinakotek.* If your partner successfully offers a related word within the time frame, he or she earns a gold star or a prize from a grab bag. If not, or when the time is up, you will do the same with your partner's list.

Was macht sie?

Lebendige Sprache

A   Tennis/Squash

Schönhagen

Tenniscenter Hochsolling
2 Hallen- und 2 Außenplätze,
Tel.: 05571 6116 oder 0174 9604945

Silberborn

Außenplätze
April bis Oktober, Vermittlung Verkehrsamt,
Tel.: 05536 223

C Camping

Bad Gandersheim

DCC Kurcamping-Park
Tel.: 05382 1595

E   Fahrradverleih

Bad Karlshafen

Campingplatz Bad Karlshafen
Tel.: 05672 710

2-Rad Lantelme
Bergstr. 14, Tel.: 0 56 72 / 20 85 Fahrrad- und MTB-
verleih, Service u. Verkauf, Trekking; Mountainbike

G   Burgen, Museen

Adelebsen

**Museum für Steinarbeit/
Verein für ländliches Alltagsleben e. V.**
Öffnungszeiten April – Oktober: So.: 15.00 – 17.30
Uhr. Für Gruppenführungen jederzeit nach Anmel-
dung: Tel.: 05506 7801

Bad Gandersheim

Museum der Stadt im Rathaus
Für Gruppenführungen Anmeldung:
Tel.: 05382 73-700.
Die neuen Öffnungszeiten: Di. – So.: 15.00 – 17.00
Uhr, zusätzlich Fr. – So.: 10.30 – 12.30 Uhr

I Reiten

Aerzen

Reiten für Kinder und Erwachsene,
Reiterhof „Weserbergland"
Aerzen-Reinerbeck, Tel.: 05154 96295

B  Freizeitparks

Salzhemmendorf-Benstorf

Rastiland
mit Rafting, Wildwasserbahn, Achterbahn, Gokarts
uvm. Geöffnet 2006: 1. 4. – 18. 4. tägl. von 10 – 17
Uhr; 19. 4. – 30. 4. nur Sa. und So.: 10 – 18 Uhr;
1. 5. – 31. 8. tägl. 10 – 18 Uhr; 1.9. – 30. 9. jeweils
Mi./Sa./So. 10 – 18 Uhr; 1. 10. – 3. 10. tägl. von 10
– 18 Uhr, 4. 10. – 15. 10. nur Sa. und So. 10 – 18
Uhr; 16. 10. – 29. 10. tägl. 10 – 17 Uhr;
www.rasti-land.de, Tel.: 05153 6874

D   Bootsverleih

Alfeld

Geführte Kanutouren
Verleih, Tel.: 05181 806422 oder
0171 2816422, www.goesseltours.de

Bad Karlshafen

Kanu-Schumacher
Kanuwandern auf Diemel und Weser mit Boots-
und Personentransfer. Infos: 05642 7682 oder
www.kanu-schumacher.de

F   Tierparks

Bad Pyrmont

Tierpark Bad Pyrmont
Tiere aus allen Erdteilen. Ganzjährig geöffnet.
Tel.: 0 52 81 / 25 39,
www.tierpark-badpyrmont.de

H   Ballonfahrten

Coppenbrügge

Ballonteam Perspektive
Wir starten ab Hameln, Pyrmont, Bodenwerder etc.,
Tel.: 05156 7179, www.ballon-perspektive.de

Moringen

Awis - Ballonfahrten - Busreisen
Die höhere Art des Reisens. Tel.: 0171 7983850

J Minigolf

Neuhaus im Solling

Moderne 18-Loch-Bahnengolfanlage
April bis Oktober, am Haus des Gastes,
Tel.: 0 55 36 / 10 11. Öffnungszeiten laut Aushang

J Match the places for recreational activities or facilities that you can use with their respective descriptions. People. . .

_____ 1. . . . go there to admire different kinds of animals.

_____ 2. . . . can rent different kinds of bikes.

_____ 3. . . . enjoy rafting and riding go-karts.

_____ 4. . . . call 0515496295 and make reservations for this activity.

_____ 5. . . . can play this sport in two towns outdoors or indoors.

_____ 6. . . . can stay overnight in this park.

_____ 7. . . . are lifted into the air from several locations.

_____ 8. . . . enjoy playing this recreational sport by hitting a ball with a putter.

_____ 9. . . . can visit exhibits in two towns.

_____ 10. . . . are on the water in rented canoes.

K Pick three of the listed places and imagine going there. Give reasons why you would like to go there and why you would like to be involved with this activity.

_____

_____

_____

_____

_____

Sprichwort

In der Abwechslung liegt das Vergnügen.
Variety is the spice of life.

Symtalk

L Ergänze die richtigen Wörter auf Deutsch! *(In the space, write the correct word in German.)*

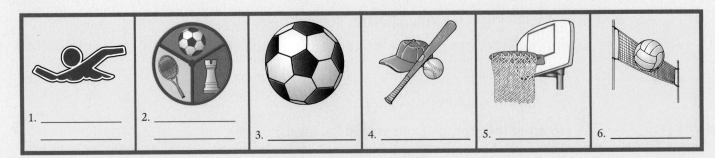

1. _____

2. _____

3. _____

4. _____

5. _____

6. _____

M Sag die Sätze! Dann schreib sie auf Deutsch! *(Say the sentences, then write them in German.)*

1.

_____

2.

_____

3.

_____

4.

_____

5.

_____

N **Mit einem Klassenkameraden, stell die Frage oder gib die Antwort!** *(With a partner, ask the question or give the answer. Then, write the dialogue.)*

1.

_____

Nein, _____

_____

2.

_____

Nein, _____

_____

3.

_____

Nein, _____

4.

_____

Nein, _____

_____

Kreuzworträtsel

Note: ß = SS

Waagerecht

2. game with a black and white ball
6. game
9. game with a racquet and a ball
12. *Ich _____ ins Museum.*
13. *_____ Sportart treibst du?*
14. beach
15. game with a net and a ball

Senkrecht

1. *Ich _____.* (what you do with a book)
3. game with a hoop and a ball
4. *Ich _____ Ski.* (what you do with skis)
5. *Ich _____.* (what you do on a ranch)
7. *Ich _____.* (what you do at a dance)
8. *Was _____ du gern?*
10. *Ich _____.* (what you do in the water)
11. *_____ gehst du?*
12. *Was machst du _____?*

UNIT 19

Das Einkaufen

Shopping

EURO
die neue Währung

EURO
EYPO

Die Einführung der Europäischen Währung

Vokabeln

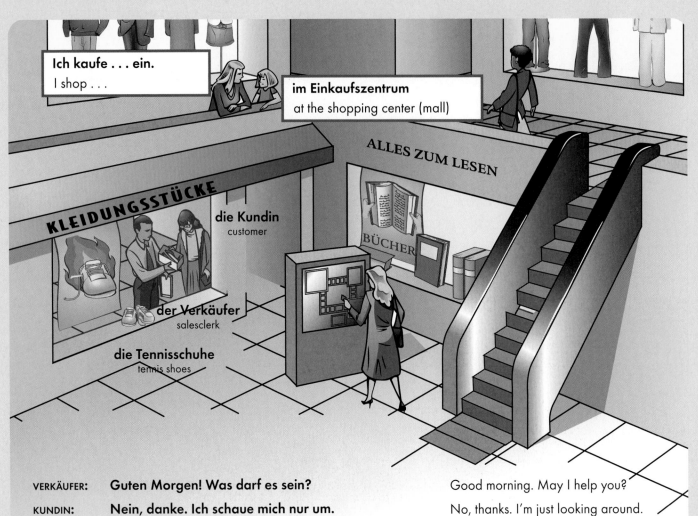

Ich kaufe . . . ein.
I shop . . .

im Einkaufszentrum
at the shopping center (mall)

ALLES ZUM LESEN

KLEIDUNGSSTÜCKE

die Kundin
customer

BÜCHER

der Verkäufer
salesclerk

die Tennisschuhe
tennis shoes

VERKÄUFER:	**Guten Morgen! Was darf es sein?**	Good morning. May I help you?
KUNDIN:	**Nein, danke. Ich schaue mich nur um.**	No, thanks. I'm just looking around.

❀❀❀❀❀

VERKÄUFER:	**Guten Morgen! Was darf es sein?**	Good morning. May I help you?
KUNDIN:	**Ja, bitte. Ich möchte ein Buch kaufen.**	Yes, please. I'd like to buy a book.
VERKÄUFER:	**Gut. Unsere Auswahl ist sehr groß.**	Fine. Our selection is very big.

❀❀❀❀❀

RUTH:	**Wohin gehst du?**	Where are you going?
RÜDIGER:	**Zum Einkaufszentrum.**	To the shopping center.
RUTH:	**Was kaufst du dort?**	What are you going to buy there?
RÜDIGER:	**Tennisschuhe.**	Tennis shoes.

im Angebot	on sale	**kaufen**	to buy; *ich kaufe*
zum Verkauf	for sale	**einkaufen**	to shop; *ich kaufe . . . ein*
der Preis	price	**kosten**	to cost; *er/sie/es kostet*

im Geschäft
at the store

die Kassiererin
cashier

der Kunde
customer

das Angebot
special offer

das Geld
money (bills or paper money)

die Kasse
cash register

das Kleingeld
change (coins)

die Compact Disc; die CD
compact disc, CD

KUNDE:	**Wie viel kostet diese CD?**	How much does this CD cost?
KASSIERERIN:	**Sie kostet €12.***	It costs 12 euros.
KUNDE:	**Das ist etwas teuer!**	That's a little expensive!
KASSIERERIN:	**Nein, das ist billig.**	No, that's cheap.
KUNDE:	**Also, gut. Ich kaufe die CD. Hier ist das Geld.**	Well, O.K. I'll buy the CD. Here's the money.
KASSIERERIN:	**Danke schön. Da ist Ihr Kleingeld.**	Thank you very much. There's your change.

*In German, a sum of money uses the singular. Example: *Sie kostet 12 Euro.*

die Verkäuferin
vendor

die Pfirsiche
peaches

die grünen Bohnen
green beans

auf dem Markt
at the market

VERKÄUFERIN:	**Noch etwas?**	Anything else?
KUNDE:	**Ja, drei Tomaten, fünf Pfirsiche und grüne Bohnen. Das ist alles.**	Yes, three tomatoes, five peaches, and green beans. That's all.

Übungen

A Match the items for sale with the stores in which they can be found.

A		B
1. _____	Tennisschuhe	A. market
2. _____	grüne Bohnen	B. shoe store
3. _____	Compact Discs	C. furniture store
4. _____	Stühle und Tische	D. stationery store
5. _____	Kulis und Hefte	E. music store

B Ergänze jeden Satz der Abbildung nach. *(Using the picture cue, complete each sentence.)*

1. Ich esse _____ gern.

2. Frau Huber kauft viel Obst auf dem _____.

3. Ich gehe zum _____.

4. Hier ist Ihr _____, Herr Maier.

5. Die CD ist billig. Sie _____ 12 Euro.

C **Choose the expression from the following list that completes each sentence correctly.**

billig   kaufen   Euro   Geschäft   Kasse

Lorenz geht zu einem _____. Er möchte eine CD _____. Da ist
eine gute CD zu 10 _____. Das ist nicht teuer. Das ist _____.
Er geht mit *(with)* der CD zur _____.

ein Einkaufszentrum

Was kauft sie hier?

D Wähle die richtige Antwort! *(Choose the correct answer.)*

1. If you see the sign *im Angebot,* how would you expect the price of this object to be?
   A. billig
   B. teuer
   C. schön
   D. grün

2. What do you reply if the cashier says, *"Das macht 15 Euro."*
   A. Wo ist das Geschäft?
   B. Ich kaufe auf dem Markt ein.
   C. Hier ist das Geld.
   D. Was kaufst du dort?

3. What do you get back if you give the cashier too much money?
   A. Auswahl
   B. Kasse
   C. Markt
   D. Kleingeld

4. Who helps you find what you need?
   A. der Verkäufer oder die Verkäuferin
   B. der Kunde oder die Kundin
   C. der Kassierer oder die Kassiererin
   D. der Landwirt oder die Landwirtin

5. What do you say if you want to find out about the price?
   A. Wie viel Uhr ist es?
   B. Wie viel kostet das?
   C. Wie viel Geld hast du?
   D. Wie viel ist neun und zwölf?

E Write the English for the following:

1. Ich kaufe die Tennisschuhe.

_____

2. Du kaufst sieben Pfirsiche.

_____

3. Sie kauft eine CD. (**Hint:** *Sie* refers to *die Kundin.*)

_____

F Wähle die richtige Antwort zu jeder Frage! *(Choose the correct answer for each question.)*

1. Noch etwas?
   A. Ja. Ich spiele Fußball.
   B. Ja. Ich möchte ein Buch kaufen.
   C. Ja. Ich habe Geld.
   D. Ja. Ich kaufe im Geschäft ein.

2. Warum gehst du auf den Markt?
   A. Ich möchte Bananen und Birnen kaufen.
   B. Der Markt ist teuer.
   C. Ich habe Kleingeld.
   D. Ich gehe mit.

3. Ist die CD teuer?
   A. Ja. Das ist eine CD.
   B. Sie ist im Geschäft.
   C. Nein. Sie ist schön.
   D. Nein. Sie ist billig.

4. Wie viel kosten die Tennisschuhe?
   A. Eine Auswahl.
   B. Eine Kasse.
   C. Viel Geld.
   D. Viele Pfirsiche.

5. Was darf es sein?
   A. Ich habe Kleingeld.
   B. Nein, das ist nicht billig.
   C. Ich möchte grüne Bohnen kaufen.
   D. Das kostet viel Geld.

G **Ali is looking at clothing in a large department store. Complete his conversation with the salesclerk.**

VERKÄUFER:	Guten Tag. Was darf es (1.) _____.
ALI:	Ich (2.) _____ _____ nur _____.
VERKÄUFER:	Alle Hemden, Hosen, Mäntel und Schuhe, sind nun reduziert. Alles ist heute im (3.) _____.
ALI:	Danke schön. Oh . . . diese blaue Hose, wie viel (4.) _____ sie?
VERKÄUFER:	Sie kostet € 59.
ALI:	Das ist noch etwas (5.) _____. Ich kann sie nicht kaufen.

H Zum Sprechen. **Think of three things you would like to buy (for example, a notebook, a shirt, a sandwich). You now need to know the price of each item. Ask your speaking partner how much each one costs:** *Wie viel kostet das?* **He/she should tell you a specific price. Then react to the price by saying:** *Das ist teuer* **or** *Das ist billig* **or** *Das ist gut.*

I Du bist dran! **You and your partner are going to play store today. Decide who will be the customer and who will be the salesclerk. The salesclerk will greet the customer and ask to help. The customer will say that he/she would like to buy an item. The salesclerk will mention the large selection of those items. The customer will ask how much one costs. The clerk will proceed with the purchase. The clerk will finally thank the customer and say good-bye. Use a real item such as a** *Lineal, Heft, CD, Pulli, Kuli,* **or** *Apfel* **and use play money in your cash register. Hang the store owner's sign above the store, e.g.,** *Ebis Geschäft, Bernds Ecke,* **or** *Maries Markt.* **Take turns being clerk/vendor and customer.**

Lebendige Sprache

SCHUHE UND LEDERWAREN

Deichmann-Schuhe GmbH & Co. KG
57076, Hauptmarkt 11
Tel. 0271 / 4 88 90 93

flac
57072, Bahnhofstraße 30
Tel. 0271 / 2 38 05 80
Mo. - Sa. 10 - 19 Uhr
Lifestyle Trendshop
bags, clothes, shoes und accessoires

SPORTARTIKEL, FREIZEIT UND ZWEIRAD

Intersport Langenbach
57076, Hauptmarkt 14-15
Tel. 0271 / 4 65 88
Mo. - Fr. 9.30 - 18.30, Sa. 9.30 - 15 Uhr
Die Nr. 1 in Sachen Sport – Ihr kompetenter
Partner rund um den Sport

BÜCHER UND ANTIQUITÄTEN

Buchhandlung Am Kölner Tor
57072, Sandstraße 1
Tel. 0271 / 2 32 25 12
Mo. - Fr. 9 - 19, Sa. 9 - 16 Uhr
Bücher – Lesen ist Leben! –
Erleben Sie uns.

GLAS, KERAMIK

Casa Leonardo
57072, Am Bahnhof 40 – City-Galerie

Daub + Daub gegenüber
57076, Hauptmarkt 10
Tel. 0271 / 4 31 23

WMF
57072, Am Bahnhof 40 – City-Galerie
Tel. 0271 / 2 38 23 66

KAUFHÄUSER

Karstadt Warenhaus AG
57072, Kölner Straße 41
Tel. 0271 / 59 88-0
Mo. - Fr. 9.30 - 19 Uhr, Sa. 9 - 17 Uhr
Warenhaus im Herzen von Siegen mit
über 9000 qm Verkaufsfläche

UNTERHALTUNGS-ELEKTRONIK

Beitzel Fernsehmeister
57072, Löhrstraße 36
Tel. 0271 / 23 06 00
Mo. - Fr. 8 - 22 Uhr (Notdienst)
Erstklassig hören und sehen

SPIELWAREN

Emil Weber KG
57072 Siegen, Kornmarkt 14-16
Tel. 0271 / 2 30 63-0
Mo. - Fr. 9 - 18.30, Sa. 9 - 14 Uhr
Die Spezialisten für Märklin-Eisenbahnen
und Modellbahnzubehör

INSTRUMENTE

Musikhaus Horn GmbH & Co. KG
57072, Friedrichstraße 2
Tel. 0271 / 5 13 17

Musikladen Krause
57072, Am Bahnhof 40 – City-Galerie
Tel. 0271 / 2 30 69-0

Pianohaus Füllengraben
57072, Frankfurter Straße 31
Tel. 0271 / 5 51 67

WOHNEN UND WOHNACCESSOIRES

Ambiente
57072, Sandstraße 31 – Reichwalds Ecke
Tel. 0271 / 50 17 67
Mo. - Fr. 10 - 19, Sa. 10 - 16 Uhr
Individuelle Einrichtungen, ausgewählte
Accessoires, Präsente

COMPUTER UND BÜROTECHNIK

Bits & Bytes
57076, Weidenauer Straße 159
Tel. 0271 / 33 84 60

Hees Bürowelt
57072, Hagener Straße 67
Tel. 0271 / 48 81-0
Mo. - Fr. 8 - 18, Sa. 9 - 13 Uhr
Bürotechnik, Büroeinrichtung, IT-System-
haus, Bürobedarf, EDV-Zubehör

BLUMEN

Blumenreich
57072, Herrengarten 2
Tel. 0271 / 2 31 88 80
Mo. - Fr. 9 - 18.30, Sa. 9 - 16 Uhr
Blumen für alle privaten und
geschäftlichen Anlässe

UHREN UND SCHMUCK

Die Goldschmiede
57076, Hauptmarkt

Juwelier Christ
57072, Am Bahnhof 40 – City-Galerie
Tel. 0271 / 2 38 23 94

Juwelier Grimm
57076, Hauptmarkt 8, Tel. 0271 / 4 18 40

KINDERMODEN

Annabell Kindermoden
57072, Kölner Straße 27
Tel. 0271 / 2 38 38 63

Schuhbidu Kinderschuhe
57072, Alte Poststraße 19
Tel. 0271 / 2 31 61 60
Mo. - Fr. 10 - 18.30, Sa. 10 - 14 Uhr
Das Kinderschuhfachgeschäft, das
keine Wünsche offen lässt.

Where can you buy these items? The stores listed below the items offer certain products for purchase. Read the description and write the appropriate letter that refers to these stores. In this/these store(s) you can buy...

____ 1. children's clothing

____ 2. toys such as model trains

____ 3. office supplies and computers

____ 4. clocks and jewelry

____ 5. musical instruments

____ 6. shoes and other leather goods

____ 7. living room furniture and accessories

____ 8. television and other entertainment items

____ 9. sports and leisure articles

____ 10. nearly everything at this department store has a 9000 square meter shopping area

____ 11. glass and ceramic products

____ 12. flowers for private and business occasions

____ 13. books and antique items

K **Select one of these stores and write at least three reasons why you would want to shop there.**

_____

_____

_____

Sprichwort

Wer den Pfennig nicht ehrt, ist des Talers nicht wert.

He who doesn't value the penny doesn't deserve the dollar.

Symtalk

L Ergänze die richtigen Wörter auf Deutsch! *(In the space, write the correct word in German.)*

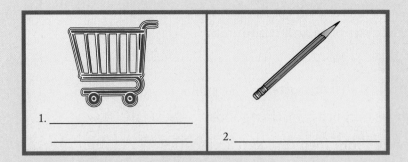

1. _____

2. _____

M Sag die Sätze! Dann schreib sie auf Deutsch! *(Say the sentences, then write them in German.)*

1. _____

2. _____

3. _____

4. _____

5. _____

N Mit einem Klassenkameraden, stell die Frage oder gib die Antwort! *(With a partner, ask the question or give the answer. Then, write the dialogue.)*

1.

_____   _____ .

2.

_____   _____ .

3.

_____   _____ .

4.

_____   _____ .

5.

_____   _____ .

Kreuzworträtsel

Note: ß = SS

Waagerecht

3. place that sells mostly fruits and vegetables
6. register to hold money
8. price
9. _____ *kaufe auf dem Markt ein.*
10. *grüne* _____
11. *Ich* _____ *eine CD.*
12. change
14. needed to buy things

Senkrecht

1. expensive
2. *Die Auswahl ist* _____. (large)
4. selection
5. _____ *gehst du?*
6. *Wie viel* _____ *das Obst?*
7. shopping
8. peaches
10. cheap
13. _____ *Kunde* (the customer)

UNIT 20

Das Reisen und der Verkehr
Travel and Transportation

Vokabeln

Wie reist du?
How do you travel?

Ich reise mit dem Flugzeug.
I travel by plane.

Ich fahre mit dem Auto.
I travel by car.

Ich fahre mit dem Bus.
I travel by bus.

Ich fahre mit dem Schiff.
I travel by ship.

Ich fahre mit dem Zug.
I travel by train.

Extra

fliegen	to fly
Ich fliege.	I fly.

auf dem Flughafen
at the airport

die Angestellte
clerk, agent

der Reisepass
passport

der Koffer
suitcase

der Reisende
traveler

der Schalter
ticket counter

ANGESTELLTE:	**Ihren Reisepass, bitte?**	Your passport, please?
REISENDER:	**Er ist in meinem Koffer.**	It's in my suitcase.
ANGESTELLTE:	**Sie brauchen ihn, wenn Sie bei der Passkontrolle ankommen.**	You'll need it when you arrive at passport control.
REISENDER:	**Also, gut. Warten Sie, bitte! . . . Hier ist mein Reisepass. Wo steht das Flugzeug?**	Well, O.K. Wait, please. . . Here's my passport. Where is the plane?
ANGESTELLTE:	**Am Flugsteig 20. Dort drüben, rechts. Gute Reise!**	At gate 20. Over there, to the right. Have a nice trip!

der Angestellte
clerk

die Fahrkarte
ticket

die Reisende
traveler

der Fahrplan
schedule

REISENDE:	Um wie viel Uhr fährt der nächste Zug nach Berlin?	At what time does the next train for Berlin leave?
ANGESTELLTER:	Um zwölf Uhr. Hier ist der Fahrplan.	At twelve o'clock. Here's the schedule.
REISENDE:	Danke. Ich möchte eine Rückfahrkarte, zweite Klasse.	I'd like a round-trip ticket, second class.
ANGESTELLTER:	Hier ist Ihre Fahrkarte. Das macht € 120.	Here's your ticket. It's € 120.

auf der Straße
on the street

der Bus
bus

HERR MENDELSSOHN:	Entschuldigen Sie! Wie komme ich zum Hotel Krone?	Excuse me. How do I get to Hotel Krone?
FRAU SCHUBERT:	Fahren Sie mit dem Bus Nummer 2 und steigen Sie am Park aus! Das Hotel ist links.	Take bus number 2 and get off at the park. The hotel is on the left.

Übungen

A **Match the German with the English.**

	A		B
1. _____	Gute Reise!	A.	Excuse me.
2. _____	Entschuldigen Sie!	B.	Over there, to the right.
3. _____	Sie brauchen einen Reisepass.	C.	The plane is at the gate.
4. _____	Zweite Klasse, bitte.	D.	Here's a schedule.
5. _____	Dort drüben, rechts.	E.	Get off at the park.
6. _____	Steigen Sie am Park aus.	F.	You need a passport.
7. _____	Ich möchte eine Rückfahrkarte.	G.	Second class, please.
8. _____	Es ist links.	H.	Have a nice trip.
9. _____	Hier ist ein Fahrplan.	I.	I'd like a round-trip ticket.
10. _____	Das Flugzeug steht am Flugsteig.	J.	It's on the left.

B **Wie reist du? Ergänze die Sätze auf Deutsch!** *(How do you travel? Complete each sentence in German.)*

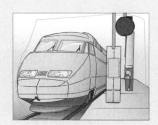

1. Ich reise _____.

2. Ich reise _____.

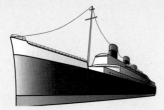

3. Ich reise _____.

4. Ich reise _____.

5. Ich reise _____.

der Fahrplan

Zeit		Zuglauf		Ziel	Gleis	Hinweis
16 09	RE	Langen-Darmstadt	Bensheim-Weinheim	MANNHEIM	13	
16 15	ICE	Fulda-Kassel-Wilhelmsh.	Göttingen-Braunschweig	BERLIN OSTBF	9	
16 15	RE	Ffm Süd	Eberbach-Heilbronn	STUTTGART	1a	
16 16	S9			AIRPORT/AEROPORT	20	✈
16 19	IC	Aschaffenburg	Würzburg-Nürnberg	PASSAU	6	
16 22	IR	Friedberg-Gießen	Marburg-Treysa-Wabern	HAMBURG-ALTONA	12	
16 26	RE	Ffm Süd-Offenbach	Hanau-Wächtersbach	FULDA	7	
16 30	RB	Ffm Süd-Ffm Ost		HANAU	8	
16 31	RB	F-Höchst-Niedernhausen		LIMBURG	2	
16 35	RE	Ffm Süd-Offenbach	Hanau-Aschaffenburg	WÜRZBURG-NÜRNBG	5	
16 42	RB	Ffm Süd-Offenbach		WÄCHTERSBACH	9	

Im Tiefbahnhof verkehren weitere S - Bahnlinien S 8,

Sie kaufen Fahrkarten.

der Zug

Wähle die richtigen Antworten! *(Choose the correct answers.)*

1. Where do you find a train?
   A. auf dem Flughafen
   B. auf dem Bahnhof
   C. bei der Passkontrolle
   D. auf der Straße

2. What do you ask if you want to buy a round-trip ticket?
   A. Ich möchte eine Fahrkarte.
   B. Ich möchte einen Reisepass.
   C. Ich möchte eine Passkontrolle.
   D. Ich möchte eine Rückfahrkarte.

3. What do you look at to find the times when trains, buses, and planes arrive and leave?
   A. der Fahrplan
   B. der Bahnhof
   C. der Flughafen
   D. der Koffer

4. Where at the airport do you go to ask for information and to check your luggage?
   A. das Flugzeug
   B. die Straße
   C. der Schalter
   D. die Passkontrolle

5. If you don't want a first-class ticket, what do you say?
   A. Hier ist der Fahrplan.
   B. Bus Nummer 2.
   C. Dort drüben, rechts.
   D. Zweite Klasse.

Schreib die Wörter richtig! *(Unscramble the words.)*

1. GIUFLESTG _____

2. FFKORE _____

3. FHARPLNA _____

4. CTRLSAHE _____

5. HFBAOHN _____

Sie sitzt im Zug.

Sie steigen ein.

Lies den Absatz und beantworte dann die Fragen! *(Read the paragraph and then answer the questions.)*

Das Wetter ist heute Morgen warm und sonnig. Bettina und Peter sind am Schalter im Hamburger Bahnhof. Sie sind glücklich. Sie *machen eine Reise* nach Köln. Peter *bleibt* bei den Koffern und Bettina kauft zwei Fahrkarten. Dann gehen sie zum *Bahnsteig,* wo der Zug steht. Die Freunde *steigen ein.* Im Zug sitzt Bettina am Fenster und Peter findet einen *Platz am Gang.* Auf der Reise sprechen sie von ihrem *Besuch* bei Bettinas Verwandten in Köln. Am Mittag kommen sie im Kölner Bahnhof an. Sie steigen aus.

machen eine Reise	are taking a trip
bleibt	stays
der Bahnsteig	platform
steigen ein	climb on board
der Platz am Gang	seat on the aisle
der Besuch	visit

1. Wie ist das Wetter?
   A. schön
   B. schlecht
   C. nicht gut
   D. kalt

2. Wo sind Peter und Bettina?
   A. auf dem Flughafen
   B. im Flugzeug
   C. im Auto
   D. auf dem Bahnhof

3. Wie viele Fahrkarten kauft Bettina?
   A. eine
   B. zwei
   C. drei
   D. vier

4. Wo steht der Zug?
   A. am Fenster
   B. am Bahnsteig
   C. am Schalter
   D. am Gang

5. Wo steigen Bettina und Peter aus?
   A. in Hamburg
   B. in Innsbruck
   C. in Köln
   D. in Genf

F Complete the analogies.

1. kaufen: Kunde = _____ : Reisender
2. Bahnhof: _____ = Flughafen: Flugzeug
3. Schiff: Ozean = Bus: _____
4. Flugsteig: Flughafen = _____ : Bahnhof

G Zum Sprechen. Look at the pictures of a bus, an airplane, a car, a ship and a train. Ask your speaking partner what each one is: *"Was ist das?"* He/she will answer. Then you get to ask him/her, *"Wie reist du?"* as you point to a specific picture. He/she will answer again.

H Du bist dran! With a partner act out the last dialogue *Auf der Straße*. One of you will be Herr Haydn and the other Frau Rilke. This time, however, Mr. Haydn wants to go to another destination within the city. He will substitute another name for Hotel Krone (i.e., *Hotel Berlin, Brandenburger Tor, zum Zoologischen Garten*). Mrs. Rilke will recommend a different bus number. She will finish giving directions by saying that the place is on the right. Don't forget to say thank you and you're welcome!

Sprichwort

Das Reisen bildet.
Traveling is
an education
in itself.

Lebendige Sprache

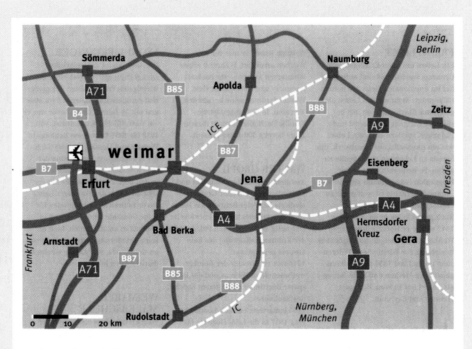

MIT PKW UND BUS:

■ Autobahn A4 Dresden-Frankfurt/
Main Abfahrt Weimar
5 km bis zum Stadtzentrum

■ Autobahn A9 Berlin-München
30 km ab Hermsdorfer Kreuz

■ B7, Kassel-Eisenach-Erfurt-
Weimar-Jena-Gera

■ B85, Bayreuth-Kulmbach-Kronach-
Saalfeld-Rudolstadt-Weimar-
Kyffhäuser (Bier- und Burgenstraße)

MIT DER BAHN:

■ InterCityExpress: Frankfurt-
Weimar-Leipzig-Dresden
InterCityExpress: Frankfurt-Weimar-
Berlin

Bahnauskunft: 11 86 1

MIT DEM FLUGZEUG:

■ Flughafen Erfurt-Bindersleben
(25 km)
■ Flughafen Leipzig (120 km)
■ Flughafen Frankfurt (300 km)
■ Flughafen Weimar-Umpferstedt
(zugänglich der allgemeinen Luftfahrt
bis 2 t Gesamtmasse)

UNTERWEGS MIT DEM REGIONALVERKEHR DER DEUTSCHEN BAHN:

Für Ihre Ausflüge in Weimars Um-
gebung können Sie kostengünstige
Angebote der Deutschen Bahn nutzen.
Informieren Sie sich über die
Geltungsdauer.

Hopperticket:
Hin- und Rückfahrt
Entfernung bis 50 km einer individuell
festgelegten Strecke
Preis Ticket 4,50 EUR
Thüringenticket:
Beliebig freie Fahrten für bis zu 5 Personen
oder Eltern/ Großeltern oder Eltern-
/Großelternteile mit eigenen Kindern bis 14
Jahre ohne Kilometerbegrenzung
Preis Ticket 26,00 EUR

Mit dem ICE nach Weimar

I **Look at the map and description for traveling to various places starting from the city of Weimar. Note: *PKW* = car, *Bahn* is the same as *Zug*.**

1. How far is Weimar to the Erfurt-Bindersleben airport?

   _____

2. In which direction would you drive to go from Weimar to Rudolstadt?

   _____

3. How much does a *Thüringenticket* cost?

   _____

4. Which highway would you take to drive from Weimar to Eisenberg?

   _____

5. What kind of train can you take to go from Weimar to Dresden?

   _____

6. Which of these two cities is located closer to Weimar: Naumburg or Bad Berka?

   _____

7. If you were to go a distance up to 50 kilometers on a regional train, how much would you have to pay?

   _____

8. Where is Frankfurt located in relation to Weimar?

   _____

9. Along which *Autobahn* (freeway) is Sömmerda located?

   _____

10. What is the name of the place where *Autobahn 9* and *Autobahn 4* intersect?

    _____

11. Which airport is farther away from Weimar? Leipzig or Frankfurt?

    _____

12. How many available parking spots does the *Beethovenplatz* have and until what time is it open?

    _____

Symtalk

J   **Ergänze die richtigen Wörter auf Deutsch!** *(In the space, write the correct word in German.)*

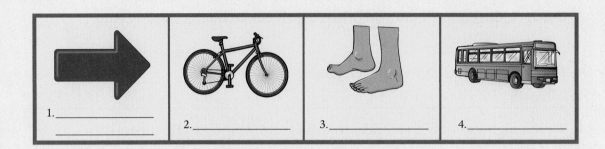

1. _____

_____

2. _____

3. _____

4. _____

K   **Lies die Sätze! Dann schreib sie auf Deutsch!** *(Read the sentences, then write them in German.)*

1.

_____

2.

_____

3.

_____

4.

_____

5. _____

L   **Beschreibe jede Szene! Auf Deutsch, bitte!** *(In German, write a description of each scene.)*

1.
_____
_____
_____
_____
_____

2.
_____
_____
_____
_____

3.
_____
_____
_____
_____

4.
_____
_____
_____
_____

Kreuzworträtsel

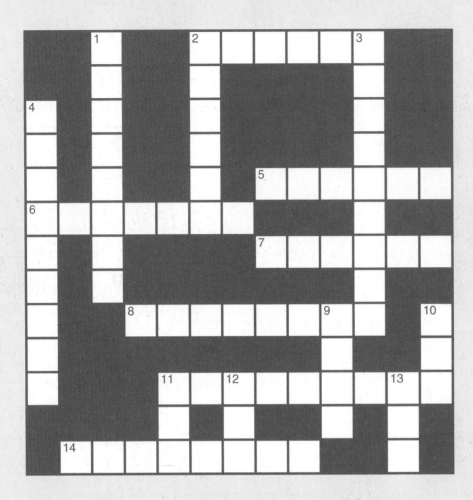

Waagerecht

2. travels on the water
5. opposite of links
6. _____ *Sie am Park aus!* (Get off at the park.)
7. traveling container for clothes
8. shows at what time a bus or plane departs and arrives
11. train platform
14. traveler = *die / der* _____

Senkrecht

1. airplane
2. *Steigst du ein? Nein, ich* _____ *aus.*
3. airplane center
4. document showing identification and citizenship
9. personal vehicle
10. travels on railroad tracks
11. public transportation
12. round trip = _____ *und zurück*
13. *Der Reisepass* _____ *in meinem Koffer.*